THE DEVELOPMENT OF MORPHOPHONEMIC THEORY

Volume 10

James Kilbury

*The Development
of
Morphophonemic Theory*

THE DEVELOPMENT

OF

MORPHOPHONEMIC THEORY

by

JAMES KILBURY

AMSTERDAM / JOHN BENJAMINS B. V.

1976

To RUDOLF ZRIMC,
whose course in Old Church Slavonic
introduced me to linguistics and aroused
my interest in morphophonemics.   .

© Copyright 1976 — John Benjamins B. V.
ISBN 90 272 0891 3 / 90 272 953 7
ISSN 0304-0720

PREFACE

This book is a revised version of my doctoral dissertation submitted to Cornell University in 1974. I am indebted to F. C. van Coetsem and L. R. Waugh for their detailed comments on the dissertation, but above all I wish to acknowledge the help I received from C. F. Hockett, who directed my graduate studies. Further thanks go to E. F. K. Koerner, the editor of this series, for bringing the book to publication. The sole responsibility for the contents is mine, however; this is especially important in regard to Hockett, since a considerable number of the opinions expressed here differ from his own.

Morphophonemics clearly is a highly controversial area of linguistics, and I have tried to be fair in presenting opposing viewpoints. To a great extent I have avoided the overt expression of my own judgements but have attempted to show them through the arrangement and selection of material. Most of all I hope that readers will find this to be a *useful* book.

My article in *Lingua* 33.235-52 (1974) is entirely superseded by this work.

Graz, 11 July 1976   J. K.

Grammarians are infatuated with the desire to multiply rationalizations. If they were to establish grammatical rules based on accurate data, instead of rationalizations, it would be much more profitable and worthwhile. But for the most part what have we read? Rationalizations of individual rules, contradictions, disputes, mutual refutations, unilateral revisions of definitions . . .—all this occasions in us disgust inasmuch as nothing of scientific value comes to hand.

Abū Ḥayyān (1256-1344)
(quoted in Glazer 1942:108)

TABLE OF CONTENTS

INTRODUCTION

The aim of this book is to provide a concise historical survey of linguistic investigation relating to the notion of morphophonemics. As such, the study is essentially historical and thus does not offer its own theory of morphophonemics. Since attention is focused on the *development* of morphophonemic theory, contemporary work in this area is not of central concern. But the study was undertaken in the hope that a better understanding of earlier work would help to clarify present-day issues.

An investigation of this nature involves special difficulties in the delimitation and specification of subject matter. A possible approach would be to adopt a particular understanding of morphophonemics and to structure the presentation and selection of material in terms of it. But such a method exhibits the weakness mentioned by R. H. Robins (1951:1):

> In dealing with the inception and history of any doctrine it is not practicable or desirable to lay down in advance definitions of key terms or of the main subject . . . .. Such definitions have their place in the exposition of a theory or in criticizing the theories of others, but can justifiably be made only after the development of quite a body of work on the subject has made possible its establishment as a science or organized system of thought and permitted a scrutiny of its methods and foundations.

The solution adopted here is to concentrate attention on actual usage of the word 'morphophonemics' and cognate terms. Of course, this approach provides a practical basis for structuring the presentation of material, but it also reflects some of the fundamental assumptions underlying the investigation. The premise that theories are neither cor-

rect nor incorrect (but instead are more or less adequate) is generally
recognized in principle but often ignored in practice by linguists; so
it may be useful to reaffirm that definitions are not "incorrect" merely
because they do not agree with the definitions offered by other linguists. It certainly is necessary to take note of cases where the usage
of a technical term departs from that followed by other linguists, but
hardly any clear terminological norms have emerged in the area of morphophonemics.[1]

This study follows the nominalist viewpoint as it is presented by
J. R. Firth (1950:42):

> In the most general terms we study language as part of the
> social process, and what we may call the systematics of phonetics
> and phonology, of grammatical categories or of semantics, are or-
> dered schematic constructs, frames of reference, a sort of scaf-
> folding for the handling of events. . . . Our schematic constructs
> have no ontological status and we do not project them as having
> being or existence. They are neither immanent nor transcendent,
> but just language turned back on itself.

Such a viewpoint encourages the tolerant attitude toward different
theories that is shown by Robins (1957:3-4):

> If the terms and categories employed by the linguist are, as
> it were, imposed on the language in the process of analysis, it
> follows that linguistic structures and systems must likewise be
> thought of not as pre-existing or discoverable in any literal sense,
> but rather as the product of the linguist in working over his mate-
> rial. No one analysis, or mode of analysis, is the only one accu-
> rate or sacrosanct, but any account of the language, in any terms,
> is an adequate statement and analysis, provided that, and to the
> extent to which, it comprehensively and economically explains what
> is heard (and read) in the language, and 'renews connection' with
> further experience of it. . . .

The nominalist position thus provides the basic motivation for em-
phasizing actual terminological usage in this study. From this perspective there is no inherent subject matter of morphophonemics aside from
usage of the term 'morphophonemics', etc., by various investigators.

---

[1] Cf. H. A. Gleason (1965:226): '"Morphophonemic" . . . is one of the
most vexed technical terms in linguistics. In no two systems of linguistic theory is it used in the same way.'

Other material, especially that involving earlier linguistic studies, is included insofar as it has a bearing on the theories that employ these terms. Biases are inevitable in judging what topics are relevant, but no single theory of morphophonemics has determined the selection. Special emphasis has been given to the views of some scholars who have been unjustly neglected by present-day linguists.

Of course, other linguists are free to take a realist position and to assume that morphophonemics has an inherent subject matter apart from particular theories; this course is followed by many linguists who actually formulate theories. But adopting the realist position in this sort of historical study would simply amount to choosing one theory and presenting all others in terms of it. Such a policy would mainly serve to make the work interesting to a narrower circle of readers and to widen the divisions that already abound in linguistics.

In view of the special prominence generative phonology enjoys in current linguistics, the discussion of this subject in Chapter VI is less extensive than one might expect, but no slight is intended. Attention is given to the early generative studies that still employ the term 'morphophonemics'; most transformationalists now reject the identification of "generative phonology" with "morphophonemics", however, and in keeping with the methodology adopted here, current work in generative phonology is not discussed. Other current linguistic theories (such as tagmemic analysis) that generally do not operate in terms of "morphophonemics" are excluded on the same methodological grounds.

The theoretical implications of the early grammatical investigations discussed in Chapter I are of great interest for modern linguistics but involve a remote area that requires the aid of specialists. On the other hand, the most recent work discussed in Chapter VI is difficult to present due to the great number of studies as well as the lack of perspective inherent in the investigation of recent history. Chapters I and VI are basically presented as background for the more detailed discussions in the other chapters.

One should note that the grouping of subject matter into chapters has been made on the basis of practical considerations and does not reflect any theory of periods in the history of linguistics.[2]

A fundamental difficulty of this study lies in that fact that it attempts to present and compare the usage of certain technical terms from various theories in isolation from other related terminology. Such an approach is undesirable since technical terms are meaningful only in relation to the other terms of the respective theories in which they are defined. But practical limitations have made it impossible to circumvent this problem.

Another problem involves the term 'morphophonemics' itself, which serves, on the one hand, as the English translation of *Morphonologie* but also distinguishes the American conception of morphophonemics from European morphophonology. In talking about the general subject matter of this work, 'morphophonemics' has been used in a broad sense that includes European morphonology; the distinction, where significant, has been spelled out explicitly.

Likewise, 'alternation' has a nontechnical sense close to 'variation' as well as a variety of differing technical usages. Later chapters, dealing with particular theories, employ 'alternation' as a technical term, but the term has also been used in its general sense.

This book presupposes a background in linguistics and familiarity with some of the scholars discussed. Since adequate illustration of the principles presented would have required a substantially longer work, a consistent policy was adopted of keeping examples to a minimum. The bibliography, on the other hand, is rather full and should enable readers to find representative applications of the various theories to real language material.

Unless otherwise indicated in the text or references, translations of Russian and Dutch passages are mine.

Single quotation marks have been used for glosses, mentioned terms, and quotations containing quotations; double quotation marks appear elsewhere. The original punctuation is retained in quotations.

---

[2] Cf. Robins (1967:61): "Any division of linguistics (or of any other science) into sharply differentiated periods is a misrepresentation of the gradual passage of discoveries, theories, and attitudes that characterizes the greater part of man's intellectual history."

CHAPTER I

CLASSICAL GRAMMATICAL TRADITIONS

The "classical" grammatical traditions are conceived in this chapter in a broad sense that includes not only Greek and Latin but also Sanskrit, Arabic, and Hebrew grammatical studies (as well as others, such as ancient Chinese, not dealt with here). It is appropriate to speak of "traditions" since we are concerned not only with the work of individual grammarians but with the cumulative products of grammatical investigation within the respective cultures; such work, after being codified by the great grammarians, acquired traditional status and retained it for relatively long periods of time.

It is not a mere gesture to take classical grammatical studies into account in dealing with a point of modern linguistic theory. Firth (1951: 69) emphasizes the undiminished value of these works:

> The great languages of the older civilizations were well served by grammarians whose eminence has not been levelled or overlaid by the thousands of grammars of modern languages which have continued to flow into schools and academies since the Renaissance with the ubiquity of the printing-press. What modern linguist would wish to find serious fault with the grammatical outlines of Pānini for Sanskrit, or of Dionysius for Greek, of Donatus and Priscian for Latin, or of Sībawayhi and Al Kalīl for Arabic? Three very different systems, the Ancient Indian, the Graeco-Roman, the Arabic, owe some of their excellence to their independence, to the absence of any international or universal grammatical dogma.

The last sentence of the preceding quotation deserves special consideration: the classical grammars did not result from the application of a given theoretical framework to the description of a language; on the contrary, the gradual emergence of a linguistic theory was concurrent with the cumulative process of description itself. While the different traditions had some influence on each other, each adapted itself to its own distinct task; and the structures of the languages themselves, rather than particular theoretical frameworks, provided what Firth (1968b:114) calls "the source of light" for the grammars:

> Widely scattered societies have treasured the classical sources of Sanskrit, Greek, Latin and Arabic over long periods, and the special grammars have been many and various, but they have not in any one tradition been utterly unlike one another, and rather suggest a constellation of systems held together by the source of light.

Since the best of these grammars are excellent descriptions suited to the structures of the respective languages, they provide a check for modern theory-building in that they show us what grammatical notions actually arose in the process of description. At the same time these works help to expose our modern preconceptions as to what a grammar must be or include.

A basic assumption of modern linguistics is that any description of a language will include analysis below the level of the word, involving units of some sort like "morphemes"; such morphological analysis is presupposed by most aspects of linguistic theory that have been included within the notions of "morphophonemics" or "morphonology". It therefore is important to realize that morphological analysis is a special feature of certain grammatical traditions that is lacking in other traditions,[1] where, consequently, some of the problems that figure most centrally in the various theories of morphophonemics—especially internal sandhi and grammatically conditioned ablaut—could not arise.

Greek and Latin

The lack of morphological analysis in the Greco-Roman tradition is quite apparent despite the morphological complexity of Greek and Latin. Robins (1957a:92) points out that the Greek grammar of Dionysius Thrax (ca. 100 B.C.) recognizes no meaningful unit smaller than the word:

One notices at once the absence of any mention of a grammatical element corresponding to the morpheme of present day grammatical analysis. The nearest approach to the conception of the bound morpheme seems to be in the distinction drawn between compound words whose parts are equivalent in shape to separate words, and those whose parts are not, but can nevertheless be recognized as recurrent elements of word formation. Morphology or word structure was not given a distinct status within grammar, and the inflectional systems of the inflected words were handled by what Hockett has called the 'word and paradigm' method, wherein one form is selected as basic (e.g. the first person singular indicative active, in verbs), and the other forms associated with it are listed after it.[2]

The framework of Greek grammar was later adapted to the description of Latin, but Robins (1951:64) finds the same type of morphology in Priscian's Latin grammar (ca. 500 A.D.):

On the word, [Priscian] declares, against modern theory, that a subdivision below the word level, into smaller but still meaningful units, is not possible (except in the case of compound words). We have seen this view held, and indeed perhaps first made explicit, in Aristotle.

A modern reader might naively suppose that it was a relatively easy matter for early grammarians to assemble the conjugations and declensions of Greek and Latin, but A. Scaglione (1970:74-75) reports that the paradigms were reduced to a manageable system only through considerable effort over a long period of time.[3] The balance of power between the opposite principles of *analogia* and *anomalia* gradually shifted in favor of the former so that greater generalizations could be stated and used as points of reference in describing exceptions.

Since the Greek and Roman grammarians did not operate with any unit comparable to the morpheme,[4] they were not directly confronted with most of the phenomena involving alternation. There obviously was no place for internal sandhi since the morphology was presented in paradigms. V. Thomsen (1927:6) also points out that the Greek grammarians took no notice of Indo-European ablaut relations, such as in *leípo, élipon, léloipa*.

The word-and-paradigm model suited Greek and Latin well in certain respects, however.[5] Robins (1957a:93) sees a special position of the word in Greek as opposed to Sanskrit:

.

> The fact that Greek linguists took the word as their starting
> point in the grammatical study of their language may be, in part at
> least, ascribed to the relative stability of the written and spoken
> forms of Greek words in their various places relative to one anoth-
> er in sentences (in marked contrast to the 'external sandhi' phe-
> nomena associated with the word in Sanskrit.

So Greek grammar had no pressing need for a theory of external sandhi. Nevertheless, we see a certain suggestion of it in the notion of
prosodía used by Thrax (according to Robins 1957a:81) to include *pathē*
'modifications', which in turn include *apóstrophos*, the 'elision of a
word final vowel before a word initial vowel following without pause'.[6]
Robins (1957a:86) notes another aspect of Thrax's grammar that touches
on morphophonemic problems:

> Thrax shifts his classification of the consonants on to morphologi-
> cal, or even morphophonemic ground. He tells us which consonants
> can be final in nouns of the three genders, though without refer-
> ring to the rather striking restriction in the number of Greek con-
> sonants that can be final in any words in the language.

Thus, classical Greek grammar devotes a certain amount of attention
to the cannonical phonetic structure of meaningful units. But the Greco-
Roman tradition generally has little or nothing to say about the problems associated with morphophonemics. Work in this area undoubtedly was
hindered by the relatively poorly developed phonetics of western anti-
quity (cf. Robins 1967:24).

The Greco-Roman tradition nevertheless is relevant to a discussion
of morphophonemic theory because it served as the basic framework for
grammatical studies in the west up until recent times, which *in part*
accounts for the fact that notions related to morphophonemics did not
appear in western grammar until rather recently. Moreover, after recognizing the fact that the Greco-Roman grammatical studies were so far re-
moved from morphophonemic concerns, we are in a better position to appreciate the contribution of non-western linguistic traditions in this
area.

Sanskrit

The absence of morphological analysis in the Greco-Roman tradition
contrasts strikingly with the emphasis on it in classical Sanskrit grammar. In a discussion of Indian grammar before Pāṇini, W. S. Allen (1953:
2) quotes the medieval philosopher Kumārila as saying, "We cannot think
of any point of time totally devoid of some work or other dealing with
the grammatical rules treating of the different kinds of roots and af-
fixes."

Of course, the emphasis on morphological analysis did not stem from
some given theoretical framework, but rather reflected the structure of
Sanskrit itself and the problems that arose in the process of describing
it. Just as the relative autonomy of the word in Greek and Latin made it
possible for grammarians to seek no smaller meaningful unit, the similarity between the effects of internal and external sandhi in Sanskrit made
it convenient for Indian grammarians to recognize morpheme-like units
(rather than words) if they were to undertake any analysis at all in
terms of units smaller than the sentence.

Distinctions of considerable theoretical interest are to be seen in
the Sanskrit grammatical terminology involving sandhi.[7] For example, the
term *prakṛti* 'basis' is applied to the form of a word in isolation, as
opposed to the term *vikāra* ('modification', 'variant') for the changed
form of a word showing the effects of sandhi in combination with other
words (cf. Allen 1953:10-11). A similar distinction at the morpheme level
is described by Robins (1967:147):

> Formal variations among functionally equivalent elements, such
> as are handled under the modern concept of allomorphs of single mor-
> phemes, were dealt with by Pāṇini morphophonemically. He set up ab-
> stract basic forms, called *sthānin* ('having a place', 'original'),
> which by the rules of morphophonological change and internal *sandhi*
> were converted into the actual morphs of the resultant words; the
> formal replacements were called *ādeśa* ('substitute'). General rules
> were given together with exceptions . . ..

Allen (1955:111-12) explicitly warns against interpreting these
terms as reflecting a "process" model in Pāṇini's grammar; such a reading
can be made since "the traditional translation of Pāṇini's terms by

'original' and 'substitute' respectively suggests a recognition that both belong to the same (phonological) level of statement; and that one is 'prior' to the other." Indeed, G. Cardona (1967:39) notes that "Pāninian rules are regularly verbless statements". A direct identification of Pāṇini's framework with any modern model raises very great problems.

But the parallels to process-model techniques in modern morphophonemic description are striking. "Classifiers" have the function of morphophonemic symbols,[8] and J. F. Staal 1965 shows that many of the statements in Pāṇini's grammar have the mathematical structure of context-sensitive rules. While we should be duly impressed by the fact that Pāṇini was able to provide a descriptively adequate account of Sanskrit sandhi, his enormous achievement lies in the creation of a highly technical and formal metalanguage to serve as his descriptive vehicle.

Pāṇini handles the phenomenon of ablaut, which eluded earlier Indian grammarians, together with sandhi. The reduced ablaut grade is taken as basic, and the normal and lengthened grades are derived from it; the latter two correspond, respectively, to *guṇa* 'secondary quality' and *vṛddhi* 'increase' (cf. Allen 1953:12-13).

All these notions of sandhi, ablaut, roots, and morphemes have become such an integral part of modern linguistics as to seem almost self-evident. But, as Thomsen (1927:5) observes, we must remember that they remain on the level of a model and are a distinctive contribution of the Sanskrit grammatical tradition:

> man muß sagen, daß die neuere Sprachwissenschaft eigentlich erst, nachdem sie mit den Indern bekannt geworden war, das Operieren mit diesen Abstraktionsbegriffen, Wurzeln und Stämmen, gelernt hat; gerade das hat ihr auch ein von der älteren Grammatik so verschiedenes Gepräge gegeben—aber eine Zeitlang allerdings derart, daß man vergessen hat, daß dies eben nur Abstraktionen sind, nicht wirkliche Tatsachen.

Arabic and Hebrew

The work of early Arab and Jewish linguistic investigators deserves
a place in any account of the classical grammatical traditions, but it
is of special relevance as background in a discussion of morphophonemic
theory. Semaan (1968:26) reports that the earliest Arabic grammar traces
back to Mesopotamia, where the East Syrians had learned grammar from the
Greeks. Rabbinical scholars in turn borrowed the framework of Arab grammar and further developed it in the description of Hebrew.[9]

But even if the Arab grammatical tradition ultimately derives from
the work of Dionysius Thrax, it adapted itself so completely to the problems of the Semitic languages that we see an approach to grammar totally
different from that of the Greek tradition. Like the Sanskrit grammarians, the Arabs were accomplished phoneticians and gave special attention
to morphological studies.

In the area of phonetics, Arab grammar developed a technical terminology for combinatory changes comparable to the sandhi of Sanskrit.[10]
The *Kitāb* of Sībawaïhi (died 793 A.D.) contains a chapter on *al-idḡām*
'phonetic assimilation' (cf. Semaan, p. 40) and employs terms like *tas-
kīn* 'omitting vowel' and *badal* 'substitution' (of one sound for another
in the same place) (34). The study of phonetics was intimately connected
with that of grammar, and Axvlediani (1966:8) sees Avicenna's treatise
on articulatory phonetics (1024 A.D.) as being virtually unique in the
older Arabic literature precisely because of its exclusion of grammatical questions.

While the earliest Arab grammarians had undoubtedly given attention
to problems of morphology, the *Kitāb* is, according to Semaan (28), the
earliest surviving work that deals with grammar in the stricter sense,
i.e. *naḥw* 'syntax' and *ṣarf* 'accidence'. Reuschel (1959:39-40) points
out that because of the central position given to syntax in Arab grammar,
"eine Formenlehre (Morphologie) in unserem Sinne (Paradigmen, Stamm- und
Wurzellehre) fehlt. Der zweite Teil des *Kitāb* behandelt vielmehr im we-
sentlichen die *Wortbildung*, wonach also Wortform und -bedeutung stets
gleichzeitig betrachtet werden."

But the understanding of morphology as word formation was rather
well suited to Arabic, and the classical grammarians did not fail to recognize the cannonical structure, normally triliteral, of roots (cf.
Reuschel, p. 40). The framework of grammars of Arabic and other Semitic
languages was bound to be shaped by the fact that lexical meaning is indicated by consonantal roots, while vowels signal grammatical relations.[11] A. F. L. Beeston (1970:31) characterizes the situation as follows:

> An English word such as 'film' is a stable sequence of four pho-
> nemes in determined order; any additional morphemes, such as the
> plural morpheme in 'films', cannot disturb that nucleus of phonemes
> without making the word lose its recognizable identity. But in Ara-
> bic, verbs and nouns are a combination of two morphological strata:
> a sequence of consonant phonemes in determined order, commonly
> called the 'root', which is the prime lexical item; and a pattern
> of vowel (and sometimes consonant) phonemes into which the root
> consonants are slotted in determined positions. Both root and pat-
> tern are theoretical abstractions, and can only be actualized in
> combinations with each other.

This principle of word formation, in turn, naturally gave rise to
the metalinguistic device described by A. S. Tritton (1973:vii-viii):

> The Arab grammarians used the root *fςl*, a real root, with its
> derivatives, as the type of all words; they called *ka:tibu* the *fa:-
> ςilu* of *ktb* not the active participle and *maktu:bu* the *mafςu:lu* in-
> stead of the passive participle. *maktabu* and *maka:nu* are the *mafςalu*
> of *ktb* and *kwn* respectively; we should call them nouns of place. In
> *maka:nu* the *w* of the root has combined with the short vowel to form
> a long one.

While the Semitic languages show certain processes comparable to
Sanskrit sandhi, their outstanding feature is the system of consonantal
roots and vocalic alternation. Since this vocalic alternation signals
grammatical relations, it exemplifies the type of phenomenon that was to
become the center of concern in the European theory of morphonology. Sanskrit, on the other hand, is marked by its automatic sandhi alternations,
which do not have grammatical function and thus typify the sort of alternation emphasized in American morphophonemics.

::   ::   ::

When western scholars finally turned their attention to problems in the area of morphophonemics and morphonology, it was largely through the influence of these non-western grammatical traditions. But as Robins (1967:146-47) observes, the Greco-Roman framework continued to dominate European grammar even after its exposure to the Semitic tradition:

> Pānini's descriptions involve the isolate identification of roots and affixes, which directly inspired the morpheme concept of present-day grammatical analysis. The study of Hebrew and Arabic had led later medieval Europe to recognize the abstract root as a constant that underlies inflexional paradigms, but the typical European model of grammatical description continued to be the one handed down by Dionysius Thrax and Priscian, a thorough-going word-and-paradigm one.

Other grammatical traditions may have taken account of alternation as a linguistic problem, but they in any case had no influence on the development of western linguistics. An early medieval Irish tradition, which developed terminology for the Celtic sandhi mutations, was kept alive for centuries but did not become known in the rest of Europe and was abandoned in the seventeenth century even in Ireland.[12]

With regard to all the early grammatical traditions, the greatest obstacle to an assessment of their contributions in relation to modern linguistics has been the dearth of modern historical studies that are aimed beyond the interests of philologists in the respective areas and that are accessible to a reasonably wide audience. One can only hope that the current corrective trend will continue.

CHAPTER II

EUROPEAN LINGUISTICS FROM
BAUDOUIN DE COURTENAY THROUGH TRUBETZKOY

Most languages exhibit alternations which must be treated somehow
in any description. So we must suppose that in the period between the
establishment of the classical grammatical traditions and the founding
of modern linguistics, many grammars were written that more or less suc-
cessfully coped with these problems according to the insight and basic
craftsmanship of their authors. These works provide us, however with no
theory of alternation.[1] A case in point is the discussion of *Sandhier-*
scheinungen (129-47) in *Die Kerenzer Mundart des Kantons Glarus in ihren*
Grundzügen dargestellt (1876) by Jost Winteler, one of the great precursors of structural linguistics. Under sandhi Winteler subsumes variation
resulting from the combination of elements or from differences of stress
(129); he works with a distinction of external and internal sandhi and
notes that the two types may overlap (129-30). But Winteler's study, re-
volutionary for its contribution to phonological theory, is still essentially traditional in its approach to alternation and gives no indica-
tion of a new theoretical insight. Although every scientific idea has
its source largely in earlier investigations, an historical study of
such an idea must take account of a principle of diminishing returns and
look for a point at which the antecedents and latencies give rise to an
articulate expression of the idea. In the case of morphophonemic theory
such a clear point of emergence is to be seen in the work of Jan Baudouin de Courtenay (1845-1929) and Mikołaj[2] Kruszewski (1851-87).

Jan Baudouin de Courtenay and Mikołaj Kruszewski

Baudouin himself indicates (1972:149³ [1895:4]) that his ideas on the subject were first "expressed, or rather noted in passing" in.his published programs of lectures for 1876-77 (1972:92ff) and for 1877-78 (114ff). These discussions are indeed very sketchy, and we must look to his *Nekotorye otdely "sravnitel'noj grammatiki" slavjanskix jazykov* [*Several Sections of the "Comparative Grammar" of the Slavic Languages*] from 1881 for his first systematic written discussion. Here he introduces a number of terms that are central to his understanding of alternations (1963 I:118-19): "coherents" (Russ. *kogerenty*) are "sounds and phonetic units in general in a bond of combinatory dependence, i.e. that accomodate each other". As an example he cites *ty* and *t'i* in Russian: nonpalatal *t* and the back vowel *y* are coherents, as are palatal *t'* and the front vowel *i*. Baudouin then uses the notion of "homogenes" (Russ. *gomogeny*), or "more or less distinct sounds of the same [etymological] origin", to define "divergents" (Russ. *divergenty*) as "homogene sounds whose differences are to be explained through presently existing anthropophonic conditions", where 'anthropophonic' refers to the physical aspect of phonetics. In other words, Baudouin continues, divergents are "variants [Russ. *vidoizmenenija*] of the same sound, conditioned by presently existing sound laws". In contrast to divergents, "correlatives" (Russ. *korreljativy*) are "anthropophonically distinct but homogene sounds whose difference cannot be explained by conditions presently in evidence"; correlatives are further distinguished depending on whether or not they are linked to particular morphological functions.

This is already a formidable assemblage of new terminology, but the same work also introduces many other technical expressions. Baudouin severely criticizes this in his later writing (1972:150 [1895:6]) and speaks of the "monstrous proportions" of his "mania for inventing new and unusual technical terms". This rejection comes from a time (1894) when Baudouin had disavowed many of his views from the earlier period. The discussion of some of this terminology can be omitted without compromising the presentation of Baudouin's basic ideas.

Nekotorye otdely. also contains an instructive concluding note, part of which is quoted here in a translation by Jakobson (1971a: 403-04):

> The ideas presented above on the way in which sound relations should be consulted are, as far as I know, completely new in linguistic literature. But they are only to a certain extent my own personal property. . . . M. Kruszewski, who has attended my lectures and taken part in my courses since 1878, conceived the idea of formulating all of that more precisely. In the introduction to his master's thesis Mr. Kruszewski developed his own thoughts on this subject more exactly and scientifically than I had done in these lectures of mine. . . . The more scientific character of Mr. Kruszewski's presentation lies in his strict logical analysis of general concepts, in his separation of these concepts into their constituent parts, in the specification of the necessary features of the diverse alternations and in the general logical coherence of his whole system. It is similarly to Mr. Kruszewski's credit that he is striving in this way to elicit real phonetic laws, i.e. laws to which there would be no exceptions. Only since these ideas have been formulated and presented so graphically by Mr. Kruszewski, their further development and elaboration are possible.

Baudouin indicates specifically (1963 I:126) that Kruszewski was responsible for introducing certain terms, including 'phoneme' and 'correlation', which will be discussed below.

The master's thesis to which Baudouin alludes is Kruszewski's *K voprosu o gune: Issledovanie v oblasti staroslavjanskogo vokalizma* [*On the Question of Guna: An Investigation in the Field of Old Slavic Vocalism*] (1881a). The central part of this work is a study of Old Church Slavonic vowel alternations based heavily on the method applied only shortly before by Saussure in his *Mémoire sur le système primitif des voyelles dans les langues indo-européennes* (1879), which Kruszewski had discussed very favorably in an article of 1880. The first chapter, "Obščie zamečanija o čeredovanijax zvukov" ["General Remarks on the Alternations of Sounds"], which Jakobson (1971b:440) regards as the first presentation of a theory and classification of sound alternations in the linguistic literature, was translated by Kruszewski into German and published separately as the small book *Über die Lautabwechslung* (1881b).

The term 'phoneme', used by Saussure in his *Mémoire* to denote a distinct sound of the proto-system, is touched on briefly by Kruszewski in a footnote on page 14 of the German edition:

> Mit dem Namen *Phonem* schlage ich vor, die phonetische Einheit
> (d.h. das, was *phonetisch* unteilbar ist) zu benennen, zum Unter-
> schied vom *Laut*—der anthropophonischen Einheit.

Thus, the "phoneme" is identified with the psychological aspect of
phonetics, rather than with the anthropophonic or physical side. Kruszewski makes no systematic use of the new term in his work, however.[4]

The classification of alternations presented by Kruszewski is compact and not easily summarized. Since neither the Russian nor the German
works containing it are readily available,[5] extensive passages will be
quoted here in my translation.

Kruszewski adopts algebraic notation to make his definitions of
the various types of alternation as general as possible; parallel vertical lines separate members of an alternation.[6] The first category is illustrated by the alternation $\wedge \parallel o$ conditioned by stress in Russian
v$\wedge$dá $\parallel$ vódu (1881a:8-9; cf. 1881b:11-12):

> Let x signify the condition in which the sound s appears, and
> x_1 the condition in which s is impossible and must change into an-
> other sound. This sound, which is very close to the first, we des-
> ignate with s_1. We obtain the following distinguishing properties
> of alternations in the first category.
> 1. *The direct determinacy and presence of the alternation's
> cause.* In each alternation of any sounds $s \parallel s_1$, we find the alter-
> nation of some causes or conditions $x \parallel x_1$.
> 2. *General occurrence of the alternation.* The alternation $s \parallel
> s_1$ occurs everywhere, i.e. under the indicated conditions the
> sounds alternate *in all words* without any regard to the morphologi-
> cal categories to which these words belong.
> 3. *The necessity of the alternation.* The alternation $s \parallel s_1$
> under conditions $x \parallel x_1$ is obligatory and allows absolutely no ex-
> ceptions, i.e. the appearance of s with x_1 or s_1 with x is impos-
> sible.
> 4. *The close anthropophonic kinship of the alternating sounds.*
> The alternating sounds $s \parallel s_1$ are closely related anthropophonical-
> ly; or more exactly, they are variants of the same sound.
> The first three of these properties are decisive for determin-
> ing that an alternation belongs to the first category; the fourth
> property is not as decisive: in an alternation of the first cate-
> gory, i.e. $s \parallel s_1$, these two sounds s and s_1 *must* be anthropophon-
> ically close; in alternations of the second and third category
> they *may be* anthropophonically close.
> *One* of the first three properties is sufficient for determina-
> tion, because *all four properties are inseparable*; in other words:
> all four properties are at once peculiar to each alternation of the
> first category.

Since the sounds s and s_1 here are variants of a single sound, we may call them *divergents* [7]; we may call sound s, being primary in relation to sound s_1, the *basic divergent* [Russ. *divergent osnovnyj*, Ger. *primärer Divergent*], and sound s_1, the *derived divergent* [Russ. *divergent proizvodnyj*, Ger. *sekundärer Divergent*].

In the first category Kruszewski characterizes what we might now call subphonemic variation, but it is clear that he has also included automatic alternation, as is shown by his Russian example and also the German example of *s* ‖ *z* in *Haus* ‖ *Häuser*. No line is drawn here between phonemics and morphophonemics in the typically American sense, but perhaps his distinction is roughly that between subphonemic variation and *automatic* morphophonemic alternation, on the one hand, and nonautomatic morphophonemic (i.e. morphonological) alternation, on the other hand.[8] He intends to oppose the mechanical processes of the first category to the grammatical processes of the second, as exemplified by the alternation *u* ‖ *o* in Russian *súxoj* ‖ *sóxnut'* or *r* ‖ *z* in German *war* ‖ *gewesen* (1881a: 11-12; cf. 1881b:17-18):

> In the first category of alternations we designated the alternating sounds with the symbols s ‖ s_1 in order to indicate their close anthropophonic kinship. In the second category the alternating sounds are not so closely related; they are not variants of the same sounds, but are different sounds. So let us designate them: s ‖ z.
>
> Distinguishing properties of an alternation of the second category:
>
> 1. *Impossibility of the direct determination of the causes (conditions) of the alternation and the possibility of their absence in separate cases.* In an alternation of sounds s ‖ z the causes or conditions x ‖ x_1 may be found only by means of historical investigation. Furthermore, words with the alternation s ‖ z may not contain anything that historical investigation would reveal to us as a cause.
>
> 2. *The alternation's lack of necessity.* The appearance of the sound s under conditions x_1 and of z under conditions x is possible. (The property has been formulated approximately: actually, under conditions x_1 not the sound s but rather s_1 is possible . . .. Thus, strictly speaking, we have here not the *correlation* of sounds but their *divergence*. From this it is evident that exceptions to a *rule* of correlation are subordinate to a *law* of divergence that does not allow exceptions.)
>
> 3. *Lack of general distribution.* The alternation of sounds s ‖ z is partly tied to certain morphological categories (we designate these: f ‖ f_1).

    4. *More remote anthropophonic kinship of the alternating sounds.*
The sounds $s \parallel z$ most often are in more remote anthropophonic kin-
ship with each other.
    Of these four properties, the first two are *decisive* for the
definition of the alternation, the third is less decisive, and the
fourth still less so. The first two properties are *inseparable*.

Finally, the third category, like the second, does not involve mechanical processes of the sort found in the first category. But the
third, unlike the second, is associated with particular grammatical functions. It is illustrated by the alternation $o \parallel a$ in Russian *stroit'* $\parallel$
(za)straivat' or $u \parallel \ddot{u}$ in German *Buch* $\parallel$ *Bücher* (1881a:14; cf. 1881b:21):

    This alternation has distinguishing properties *1, 2,* and *4* in
common with an alternation of the second category; it may be identified only by its third and fifth properties, which may be thus
formulated:
    3. The alternation of sounds $s \parallel z$ is bound with the alterna-
tion of morphological categories $f \parallel f_1$.
    4. The appearance of sound s in form f_1 or of sound z in form
f_1 is impossible.
    We call alternating sounds of the second and third categories
correlatives: sound s is the *basic correlative*, and sound z^* is the
derived correlative.

Having classified alternations into these three categories Kruszewski goes on (1881a:14f; 1881b:22f) to consider how alternations arise,
and in particular, how divergents can become correlatives. Conversely,
he discusses the principle of "morphological assimilation" and shows how
alternations can be levelled out or altered analogically within paradigms
(1881a:16f; 1881b:24f).
    In his doctoral dissertation *Očerk nauki o jazyke* [*Outline of the
Science of Language*] (1883), Kruszewski continues his investigation of
alternations. Following the phonemic principle, he notes that Russian k
and k' (before front vowels) differ "only by an insignificant shading of
the same sound" (1883:37). Some instances of $\check{c}$ before front vowels involve an alternation with k (e.g. *pečenie* : *peku*, *česat'* : *kosa*,[9] etc.),
while others do not (e.g. *četa*, *isčezat'*, etc.); the accompanying front
vowels, however, *do not condition* $\check{c}$ (36). In effect he says that in order to represent $\check{c}$ as k plus front vowel it would be necessary to show
"the impossibility of these combinations or their complete absence in

the language" (40).

One must remember that at the time when Kruszewski was writing, the dominant theoretical concern in linguistics was with historical change and the notion of the *Lautgesetz*. This is the context in which Baudouin credits Kruszewski with striving "to elicit real phonetic laws, i.e. laws to which there would be no exceptions" and in which Kruszewski distinguishes "a *rule* of correlation" from "a *law* of divergence, not allowing exceptions" (both passages quoted above). The dichotomy of synchrony and diachrony is fundamental here, since both linguists see phonetic law as a synchronic notion involving active forces at work in a language, as opposed to the diachronic correspondence of sounds linking them as correlatives in a single language or as cognates in different languages.

The idea of synchronic analysis was new in linguistics, and K. Brugmann (1882) in reviewing *Über die Lautabwechslung* clearly misses Kruszewski's point when he writes 'unter "Lautabwechslung" versteht der Verfasser das, was man sonst "Lautübergang" oder "Lautwandel" nennt'.[10] But Brugmann is basically positive about the work, recommending it to "jeder Sprachforscher, der Interesse und Verständnis für die Prinzipien der Sprachgeschichte hat" and shows mildmannered restraint in pointing out the apparent gaps in Kruszewski's factual knowledge.

Kruszewski's theory of alternations is also discussed enthusiastically and applied by V. V. Radlov (1882), who suggests the term *Lautalternation*[11] for *Lautabwechslung* (60). But even Radlov uses *Gesetz* in a way that is not entirely in keeping with Kruszewski's intentions. This gives us an insight into the incredible difficulties that linguists faced in attempting to introduce notions of purely synchronic analysis at a time when linguistics was dominated by the almost exclusively historical studies of the neogrammarians and most other contemporary linguists. At the same time it suggests the confusion that surrounded the debate over the regularity of sound laws, since some scholars must have taken these to include phenomena of all sorts.

Radlov also speaks of the difficult style in which Kruszewski's booklet was written (58-59) and mentions some of the problems that kept it from finding a wider audience (58):

Für die Verbreitung des Schriftchens ist es gewiß nicht vor-
teilhaft, daß es so weit im Osten in deutscher Sprache erschienen
ist, der Verfasser war aber leider gezwungen, die Abhandlung auf
eigene Kosten in Kasan zu drucken, denn er verzweifelte, sie in
einer deutschen Zeitschrift veröffentlichen zu können, da sie ihm
aus Leipzig und Königsberg mit dem Bemerken zurückgeschickt wurde,
daß die Abhandlung sich mehr mit Methodologie als mit Sprachwissenschaft beschäftige.

Kruszewski's short life was ended by a nervous disorder that left
him incapacitated in his last years. Shortly after his death Baudouin
published a lengthy article (1888-89) that discussed Kruszewski's life
and reviewed all his published works. It is apparent that Baudouin's
ideas had changed in the years since the concluding note to *Nekotorye
otdely*. The article is a nervous mixture of praise and personal attacks
that makes disturbing reading; we are confronted with a bizarre picture
of Baudouin citing works on speech pathology while describing the dis-
integration of Kruszewski's speech and general condition (1963 I:154).
He makes an effort to link the content of Kruszewski's works to his
health (155).

Baudouin clearly attempts to regain his position from Kruszewski as
the acknowledged originator of the theory of alternations. He still has
praise for the latter's expertise in logic and his ability to organize
(150), but says that Kruszewski "received not only material to ponder,
not only facts for comparison, but also detailed conclusions and generalizations that he could not have found in such a form in the scientific
literature" (149-50). Thus, Baudouin's conviction is that Kruszewski
"merely gave a finer form to what he had already learned from someone
else" (1972:150 [1895:5]), i.e. from Baudouin[12]. Later in the work Baudouin is still more to the point (1963 I:166): "As far as the 'theory'
of alternation is concerned, it certainly did not develop independently
in Kruszewski's head. He borrowed it from me."

The influence of personality was not confined to the relationship
between Baudouin and Kruszewski, however. A. Brückner had reviewed *K voprosu o gune* in an article that showed little understanding of or appreciation for the work, and Kruszewski lashed back in an article of 1882.
Baudouin comments on this in his same article on Kruszewski (172):

There are few polemic articles that exhibit such scorn for the opponent, such arrogance, such striving to offend and personally insult, as does this reply by Kruszewski to Brückner's review . . ..

But only two pages earlier Baudouin had presented his own explanation for why the German editors had rejected Kruszewski's work for publication (170):

> The real reason for the refusal was, it seems to me, that the "theory of alternations" introduced a new basis of investigation into phonetics, and the overwhelming majority of scholars fear new principles like the plague. Introducing new ideas, one has to change and think a lot, and not everyone wants to think.

Such remarks must have offended some German linguists, and it is not unreasonable to suppose that Baudouin and Kruszewski bear a measure of personal responsibility for the fact that they received no more attention in Germany than they did.

The same article contains an analysis and criticism of Kruszewski's system of classification. Baudouin objects to calling alternants of the second type "correlatives" since there need not be any phonetic or morphological relations connecting them (164). He finds various errors and inaccuracies in Kruszewski's lists of characteristic features (165). In order to correct the theory and reestablish his position with respect to it, Baudouin published his *Próba teorji alternacyj fonetycznych* in 1894, which was followed in 1895 by an expanded German version, *Versuch einer Theorie phonetischer Alternationen*.

The introduction to the *Versuch* contains an informative account of contemporary work by other linguists, and Baudouin (1972:148 [1895:3]) identifies August Leskien's *Der Ablaut der Wurzelsilben im Litauischen* (1884) as "one of the works which most closely approaches the concept of alternations" in his own study. Leskien's book a lengthy list of forms grouped according to the ablaut (vowel alternation) series they exemplify.[13] It contains virtually no text but clearly follows Baudouin's principle that one must recognize "the *coexistence* of phonetically different but etymologically related speech sounds; only after establishing this fact can one proceed to the investigation of its causes" (149 [4]).[14]

The introduction of the *Versuch* also includes a revealing "Explanation and Defition of Certain Terms" (152-53 [9-10]):

> The *phoneme* = a unitary concept belonging to the sphere of pho-
> netics which exists in the mind thanks to a psychological fusion of
> the impressions resulting from the pronunciation of one and the same
> sound; it is the psychological equivalent of a speech sound. . . .
> *Phonetics*, as a whole, concerns all phonetic phenomena, both
> anthropophonic (whether these be of a physiological or auditory na-
> ture) and psychophonetic in which the former, sensory phenomena are
> reflected. Phonetics consists thus of two parts, of an *anthropophon-
> ic* and *psychophonetic* one.
> The *morpheme* = that part of a word which is endowed with psy-
> chological autonomy and is for the very same reason not further di-
> visible. It consequently subsumes such concepts as the root (*radix*),
> all possible *affixes*, (*suffixes, prefixes*), *endings* which are ex-
> ponents of syntactic relationships, and the like.

Baudouin notes that he had earlier interpreted the phoneme as "the
sum of the phonetic properties representing an individual unit within
either a single language or a group of languages" and that "the proposal
to use the term 'phoneme' instead of 'sound' came from Kruszewski (211-
12 [7]). But Baudouin had himself introduced the term 'morpheme'. Such
terminological advances contribute largely to the modern tone of the *Versuch.*[15] Baudouin's presentation of the terms 'alternant' and 'alternation'
(153-54 [11]) can hardly be surpassed today:

> In every language and in the speech of every individual we ob-
> serve a partial phonetic difference between etymologically identical
> morphemes. In other words, in every language there are etymological-
> ly related morphemes which differ phonetically in some of their
> parts. For example, in the etymologically related morphemes *mog-* and
> *mož-* of the Polish words *mog-ę | mož-esz* [16], the first two pho-
> nemes *m* and *o* are identical, but the final phonemes *g* and *ž* are dif-
> ferent. Such phonetically different phonemes, which are parts of
> etymologically related morphemes and which occupy the same position
> in the phonetic structure of the morphemes (in the cited example,
> the third position), we shall call *alternants*, and their relation-
> ship to each other, an *alternation*.

Traditional grammar had sought to account for alternations in terms
of *Lautübergänge*, meant in a diachronic sense. But in presenting a synchronic view of alternation Baudouin adopts a position that foreshadows
the later debates in American linguistics over analysis in terms of "allomorphs" as opposed to "morphophonemes" and the validity of "item-and-
process" as opposed to "item-and-arrangement" models[17] (154 [11-12]):

Strictly speaking, in all such cases we could consider the alternating units to be not phonemes, but morphemes, since only the
latter form semantically indivisible linguistic units. Thus, from
the point of view of the psychological reality of language, there
is an alternation between entire morphemes and their combinations
. . .. The phonetic difference between related morphemes we shall
call a *phonetic alternation*. (This alternation is connected with a
semantic alternation between the morphemes and entire words.) The
phonetic alternation of entire morphemes, however, can be reduced
to alternations of their phonemes, or the phonetic components of
the morphemes.

Baudouin attempts to escape the perspective of diachrony but
falls back into it when he must specify the nature of the "sameness" that
unites alternants; this leads to his radical identification, in effect,
of internal reconstruction with the synchronic analysis of alternations
(154 [12]):

In terms, then, of phonemes, we shall call *phonetic alternants*
or *alternating phonemes* such sounds or phonemes which differ from
each other phonetically, but are related historically or etymologically. *Phonetic alternants*, or *alternating phonemes* are, in other
words, sounds or phonemes which, though pronounced differently, can
be traced back to a common historical source, i.e. originated from
the same phoneme.

Having made this basic identification, he goes on to consider the
general criteria for establishing etymological identify (155 [13]):

Any such comparison of words and morphemes of different languages rests on the assumption that the morphemes in question are
etymologically related. The etymological relationship is established
on the basis of semasiological similarity, on the one hand, and partial phonetic similarity of the morphemes, on the other hand.
The phonetic similarity must be neither accidental nor arbitrary, but must recur in a series of morphemes comprising at least
partially the same phonemes.

Etymological relationships identified with these criteria may then
constitute either "interlingual correspondence" or the intralingual relationship of "alternation" (156 [15]).

Having made these general remarks, Baudouin is in a position to present his classification of alternation types. His exposition is difficult
to follow because of its generally vague formulations and inconsistent
applications of terminology, and it further burdens the reader by relying

on Polish examples. The summary given here is based on that by Jakobson (1971a:407):

Baudouin makes a fundamental division of alternations depending on whether they embody productive and living processes in which the conditioning of the alternation is apparent, or not. Those of the latter type are *traditional* or *paleophonetic* (1972:183f [1895:65f]), and are exemplified by ablaut in modern German, such as *e* ‖ *a* in *geb-en* | *gab* (184f). Traditional alternations serve no particular grammatical function.

If an alternation is not traditional, then an active conditioning factor is present that is either grammatical ("psychological", as Baudouin often says) or else phonetic. In the former case the alternation is a *correlation*, and the alternants are *correlatives* or *psychophonetic* alternants (175f [52f]). But Baudouin does not show how this in fact differs from ablaut. Correlation is exemplified by umlaut in German, such as *o* ‖ *ö* in *Wolf* | *Wölf-e* (plural), where the umlaut is to be identified with a particular morphological category.

If a nontraditional alternation is conditioned by phonetic factors, then it is a *divergence*, and the alternants are *divergents* (170f [42f]). This category is then subdivided: when *both* alternants are conditioned by the phonetic environment (or as we say now, when they are in complementary distribution) the divergence is *purely anthropophonic*, as with ɛ ‖ *e* in Russian *ètot* | *èti*, where the alternation is conditioned by the following consonant (palatalized before *i* and nonpalatalized before *o*); but when only *one* alternant is conditioned (e.g. in certain cases that would be regarded by American and European linguists, respectively, as involving automatic alternation or neutralization), then the alternation is *neophonetic*, or a *phonetic-etymological* divergence, as with final devoicing in German and Russian.

Baudouin adds that in cases of divergence involving "substitution", "there is a discrepancy between the intention and its anthropophonic realization: we *desire* to pronounce a given phoneme with all its properties, but we are *able* to pronounce only the modification of this phoneme, substituting possible characteristics for intended ones" (172 [45]). This explanation clearly is unsatisfactory, and Kruszewski (1881b:10) does far better when he asserts that the "impossibility" of a divergent in a given environment does not mean that the speaker *cannot* pronounce it but simply that he *does not*; it is possible only through a conscious effort.

Correlations and traditional alternations, both called 'correlations' by Kruszewski, are alike for Baudouin (1972:181 [1895:61]) in that "the degree of phonetic similarity of the alternating phonemes in such cases is completely immaterial" while the similarity is greater in a case of divergence. Furthermore, although correlations differ from traditional alternations in that only the former are productive, both lack an apparent "cause" (180 [59]; cf. 186 [71]):

> The anthropophonic causes of an alternation, its anthropophonic causal connections, lie in the history of the language and can be established only through historical-linguistic studies. At one time an anthropophonic cause was at work, but later it ceased to operate, and now it is absent.

Baudouin makes a useful distinction between *foreign* and *native* alternations (187ff [73ff]), for which examples in English (from Latin) and Russian (from Old Church Slavonic) can be cited. *Incipient* or *embryonic* alternations, finally, involve, "microscopic phenomena which can be detected only as a result of a concerted effort" (193 [81]); they are important in that "they point up the possibilities of linguistic change and provide a stimulus for further objective microscopic linguistic investigations" (194 [82]) and because they form a transition to divergents (196 [88]).

E. Stankiewicz, in his introduction to *A Baudouin de Courtenay Anthology* (26) speaks of Baudouin's "tendency to list alternants but to omit rules that would correlate and derive one set of alternants from another, more basic set", but he goes on to say that 'Baudouin's reluctance to operate with base forms and rules is understandable if we keep in mind the novelty of his theory and his apprehension that any reference to "change" or to prior and "derived" forms might be misinterpreted as meaning historical phonetic change (which happened anyway).' Stankiewicz indicates that this failure to recognize basic alternants was later corrected.

Baudouin states the principle that leads him first to reject basic and derived alternants (1972:160 [1895:20]):

> Such coexistence, or alternation, is neither phonetic change in the present nor succession in the historical sequence. It is simply the phonetic difference between etymologically related morphemes.

Essentially the same point is made by Bloomfield in his 1922 review of Sapir, and by Saussure in his *Cours* (1959:159):

> Comme toutes les lois synchroniques, celles-ci sont de simples principes de disposition sans force impérative. Il est très incorrect de dire, comme on le fait volontiers, que le *a* de *Nacht* se change en *ä* dans le pluriel *Nächte*; cela donne l'illusion que de l'un à l'autre terme il intervient une transformation réglée par un principe impératif. En réalité nous avons affaire à une simple opposition de formes résultant de l'évolution phonétique.

The point at stake in all of these passages is the difference between the synchronic analysis of an alternation and the diachronic explanation of its origin; they cannot be read as precursors of criticism against base forms in morphophonemics and generative phonology. But curiously enough it is precisely the absence of diachronic considerations that Baudouin criticizes in the descriptions of the Indian grammarians (1972:147-48 [1895:2]):

> The greatest heights here were obtained by the Indic grammarians, who developed a very refined theory of the "laws of sandhi," on the one hand and the "laws of guna" and "vṛddhi" on the other hand. But the Indic grammarians lacked a feeling for history and were unable to grasp the significance of gradual development, historical sequence, or chronology in general. As a result, their findings lay, so to speak, on a single temporal plane; everything happened simultaneously, as though there were neither a past nor present nor future. Thence also the purely mechanical character of their grammatical rules . . ..

Baudouin's later writing on alternations and related problems presents largely the same material as his earlier works. But he creates a basic bridge to the subsequent study of alternations in his *Vvedenie v jazykovedenie* [*Introduction to Linguistics*] of 1917, where he discusses the Russian alternations $\check{z} \parallel g$ in *može-* | *mogu*, $\check{z} \parallel z'$ in *vožu* | *vozi-*, and $\check{z} \parallel d'$ in *vožu* | *vodi-* and concludes that Russian in fact has three ž-phonemes (1963 II:277). This is quite close to the thinking that led to the later notion of the morpho(pho)neme.

Transmission of the Kazan School's Theory

The writings of Baudouin and Kruszewski have until recently remained largely inaccessible almost everywhere. This situation has been greatly improved by the publication of the two-volume Russian edition of Baudouin's selected works (1963). Linguists who do not read Russian should welcome *A Baudouin de Courtenay Anthology* (1972), edited and translated by E. Stankiewicz, who also supplies a useful introduction;[18] unfortunately, this volume is much shorter than the Russian edition. Kruszewski's selected works are available in the Polish edition of 1967.

The Kazan School, of which Baudouin and Kruszewski built the nucleus, has been discussed most authoritatively in papers by Jakobson (1971ab).[19] These have in turn provided the impetus for a considerable number of recent works.[20] Study of Baudouin and Kruszewski from the perspective of the history of linguistics is complicated not only by the uncertainty as to their respective individual contributions but also by the question of their relation to other—especially western—linguists.

We know that both Baudouin and Kruszewski were strongly impressed by the descriptive and essentially synchronic approach of Saussure's *Mémoire*.[21] Their work in turn was familiar to Saussure and influenced him,[22] but his *Cours de linguistique générale* of 1916 contains only a brief discussion of alternations (1960:215-20).[23] It is clear, however, that Saussure is partially responsible for spreading the ideas about alternation formulated by the Kazan School. Indeed, the new notions concerning the synchronic analysis of alternations undoubtedly reached many —if not most—western linguists through works on Indo-European, first by Saussure and then especially by Meillet, whose *Introduction a l'étude comparative des langues indo-européennes* (1903) devotes separate chapters to alternations (123ff) and the form of morphological elements (145ff); the author specifies the positions and grammatical categories in which alternations occur and distinguishes alternations with and without grammatical significance (129).

Baudouin's ideas receive extensive application in Meillet's *Les alternances vocaliques en vieux slav* (1906), whose very title is indicative
of a new orientation. But the degree to which Meillet's work was affected
by the theory of alternation is best seen in his *Grammaire de la langue
polonaise* (1921:12-24) and *Grammaire de la langue serbo-croate* (1924:32-
48), both of which devote entire chapters to the phenomenon. In his obituary of Baudouin (1930), Meillet characterizes alternation as a phenomenon that is "particulièrement clair en polonais, et en général dans les
langues slaves, mais que l'on observe presque partout et dont l'importance
est capitale". Despite the influence already evident from the *Versuch* at
this time, Meillet speaks of the mediocre attention paid to the work,
meaning, apparently, that it had not yet received the great recognition
he felt it properly deserved.

In his article "The Word 'Phoneme'" (1934), J. R. Firth draws attention to the Kazan School. After summarizing Kruszewski's classification
of alternations he mentions the English plural alternants *-s, -z, -iz* as
am example of a "morphological phoneme". This short paper undoubtedly
reached a large audience in western Europe.

But the theory of alternation was passed on directly in eastern Europe, especially through Baudouin's numerous students. One of them, L.
Ščerba speaks of the inaccessibility of Baudouin's works resulting both
from the places they were published and from the languages in which they
were written (1958:85f); this made Baudouin difficult to study and pre-
vented the realization of his full potential influence on linguistics.[24]
But his influence is quite apparent in a discussion of alternation by
Ščerba (1958:169), which could have been written by Baudouin himself,
and in Ščerba's treatise (1912; also 1958:124ff) on Russian vowels. D.
Jones (1957:5) says that he was introduced to the phoneme via Ščerba by
Baudouin.[25]

Both Ščerba (1958:14) and E. Polivanov (1968:185), another student
of Baudouin's, agree that the publication of Saussure's *Cours* in 1916
brought few ideas not already familiar to many Russian linguists. It is
perhaps noteworthy, however, that Kruszewski is given no particular cred-

it by Baudouin's other students for contributing to the theory.

V. Mathesius (1965:146), one of the prime figures in the Prague Linguistics Circle, which was formed in 1926, gives equal credit to Baudouin
and Saussure as the founders of modern linguistics. Another member of the
Prague group, H. Ułaszyn (1931:53), states that he is in general agreement with Baudouin in regard to the use of the term *Phonema*; but, using
the term *Morphonema* that he indicates having introduced in 1927 (1927:
406), Ułaszyn (1931:53) makes a further distinction:

> Ich beginne mit dem zentralen Terminus "Phonema", indem ich
> mich im allgemeinen an die Anschauung Baudouins de Courtenay halte.
> Doch zergliedere ich die meiner Ansicht nach allzu weit aufgefaßte
> Vorstellung des "Phonemas" in zwei Vorstellungen: "Phonema" und
> "Morphonema", indem ich gleichzeitig beide Vorstellungen der Vor-
> stellung "Laut" gegenüberstelle, als der Benennung einer objektiven
> Erscheinung, die mit Hilfe von Apparaten der experimentellen Pho-
> netik versinnlicht werden kann.

He defines *Phonema* as 'ein psychisches Äquivalent eines "empirischen
Lautes" und zwar eines Lautes, der als Typus empfunden wird, der sich
aber unter gewissen Bedingungen ändert' (61) but emphasizes that the study
of both *Phonemata* and their objective equivalents (*Laute*) belongs properly
to *Phonetik*. The latter is distinguished by not investigating the grammatical function of elements, as opposed to "funktionelle Phonetik oder
Morphophonematik oder Phonologie". It should be noted that this direct
identification of *funktionelle Phonetik* and *Phonologie* with *Morphonematik*
departs sharply from the understanding by Trubetzkoy.

In an effective image that compares a *Morphonema* to a brick in a
wall (58), Ułaszyn says that a study of *Phonemata* is like a classification of the individual bricks *after* the wall has been taken apart and
the bricks heaped in a pile. Once the elements are taken as *Phonemata*
they no longer stand in a relation to the *Morphemata*. *Morphonemata*, on
the other hand, are like bricks seen in their relation to other bricks
together forming a wall (58):

> (Es ist so, als wenn ich die Ziegel einer Mauer auseinanderge-
> nommen und auf einen Haufen geworfen hätte, und als wenn ich dann
> versuchte, diese Ziegel nach ihrer äußeren Ähnlichkeit zu klassifi-
> zieren, nicht aber nach ihrer Funktion.)

> Ein Morphonema aber ist der Bestandteil eines semasiologisch-morphologischen Elements der Sprache, d.h. eines Morphemas. *Ein Morphonema ist also ein Phonema in semasiologisch-morphologischer Funktion.* Daraus geht hervor, daß die Systematik der Morphonemata nur in Verbindung mit den Morphonemata möglich ist.

Ułaszyn then directly contrasts *Phonemata* with *Morphonemata* (59):

> Die Phonemata bilden also Systeme nach der äußeren Verwandtschaft, auf Grund der subjektiven Äquivalenz akustisch-artikulatorischen Prozesse . . ., die Morphonemata dagegen bilden Systeme nach der inneren, funktionellen Verwandtschaft auf Grund ihrer Homogenität innerhalb, bzw. im Zusammenhange mit den semantisch-morphologischen Einheiten, d.h. Morphemen.

This last passage recalls a remark by Baudouin in his *Versuch* (1972: 170 [1895:43]):

> But a phoneme considered apart from meaning-carrying morphemes forms a unity only as a phonetic representation, as an image embedded in memory, while the phoneme as a component of a morpheme owes its psychological unity to the etymological connection of morphemes.

It should be stressed that Ułaszyn's discussion is of particular significance because of its direct assertion that *Morphemata* are composed of *Morphonemata* rather than *Phonemata*. This question takes on particular importance within American descriptivism.

Nikolaj Sergeevič Trubetzkoy

N. S. Trubetzkoy (1890-1938) indicates in his 'Sur la "morphonologie"' that he took Ułaszyn's term *Morphonema* and used it in a different sense (1929b:85). He first defines the new area of investigation (85):

> A côté de la phonologie, qui étudie le système des phonèmes considérés comme étant les idées acoustico-motrices, significatives dans une langue donnée, les plus simples, et de la morphologie, qui étudie le système des morphèmes, la grammaire doit comprendre encore un chapitre particulier, qui étudie l'utilisation morphologique des différences phonologiques, et qui peut être applée la "*morphophonologie*" ou, en abrégeant, la "*morphonologie*".

Trubetzkoy examines the Russian words *ruka* and *ručnoj* and concludes that they contain the same morpheme in two different phonetic forms, *ruk-* and *ruč-*, which exhibit an alternation of the "acoustic ideas" (pho-

nemes) k and $\breve{c}$. These ideas then give rise to a *complex* idea of the alternation that constitutes a new linguistic unit (85):

> Ces idées, complexes de *deux ou plusieurs phonèmes suscep-*
> *tibles, en fonction des conditions de structure morphologique du*
> *mot, de se remplacer l'un l'autre au sein d'un seul et même mor-*
> *phème,* peuvent être appelées des "*morpho-phonèmes*" ou des "*morpho-*
> *nèmes*" . . ..

Trubetzkoy stresses that the alternation in *ruka* and *ručnoj* is quite
distinct from the difference of stops in *ruka* and *ruki*; the latter involves only a variation of sounds that are realizations of one and the
same phoneme conditioned by the phonetic environment—in this case, the
following vowel. A passage follows that almost seems to be addressed to
Kruszewski, since it points out a misunderstanding of his:[26] although
Russian has the alternation of k with $\breve{c}$, it is not exhibited in *kosa* and
česat' (despite their common historical origin from the roots *"kos-/*
"kes-) since it occurs only in morpheme-final position (86). This also
demonstrates the importance of distinguishing productive from unproduc-
tive alternations (87).

In another article, "Gedanken über Morphonologie", Trubetzkoy specifies the divisions within morphonology[27] (1931:161-62):

(1) die Lehre von der phonologischen Struktur der Morpheme;
(2) die Lehre von den kombinatorischen Lautveränderungen, welche
    die Morpheme in den Morphemverbindungen erleiden;
(3) die Lehre von den Lautwechselreihen, die eine morphologische
    Funktion erfüllen.

The second category is identified with the internal sandhi of Sanskrit grammar.

Trubetzkoy notes that a given alternation may not be distributed un-
iformly throughout the morphology, so that it can occur in derivation but
not inflection, for example, or in verbal but not nominal morphology (163).
The central place of morphonology in grammar and its potential for diver-
sity make it an important basis for the typological classification of
languages (163). Trubetzkoy had already emphasized (1929b:87) that each
of the Slavic languages has its own, characteristic morphonological system but that the differences are concealed when the alternations are de-

scribed in purely historical terms.

The ideas presented above are applied and further elaborated by Trubetzkoy in three of his major works, *Polabische Studien* (1929a), *Das morphonologische System der russischen Sprache* (1934), and the posthumous
Altkirchenslavische Grammatik (1954). The last work was left in incom-
plete form at the time of Trubetzkoy's death, and the long-delayed published edition includes material from his lectures of 1932-33.[28] Unfortunately, it contains the shortest discussion of morphonology of the
three works.

Polabische Studien introduces an interesting notion when it suggests
that "Das phonologische Lautbild eines veränderlichen Morphems im Sprach-
bewußtsein verschwommener und weniger bestimmt als das Lautbild eines un-
veränderlichen Morphems sein mußte" (1929a:162); the distribution of alternations in Polabian led Trubetzkoy to conclude that its root morphemes
show a progressive decrease in phonological definiteness starting from
their initial segments (163).

But the most complete work by Trubetzkoy dealing with morphonology
is *Das morphonologische System der russischen Sprache.*[29] Morphonological
processes are here divided into two categories (1934:20): *Morphemwechsel,*
"die Verbindung desselben Wurzelmorphems bald mit einem, bald mit dem
anderen Suffix- bzw. Endungsmorphem", and *Morphemänderung,*[30] "die Verän-
derung der Lautgestalt eines Morphems". Trubetzkoy is concerned with the
latter category and further divides it (20):

> Die Veränderungen der Lautgestalt eines Morphems können ent-
> weder *kombinatorisch* oder *frei* sein. Die kombinatorischen Veränder-
> ungen sind durch die äußere Lautstellung des Morphems und durch
> seine Berührung mit anderen Morphemen hervorgerufen.

In contrast, *freie Morphemänderungen* or *Alternationen* involve no
shift of the phonetic environment (cf. 1954:102); the distinction leads
back to his basic notion of the *Morphonem* (1934:30):

> Jeder Alternation entspricht im Sprachbewußtsein ein *Morphonem*
> [31], d.i. die als morphologische Einheit gedachte Gesamtheit der
> an der betreffenden Alternation beteiligten Phoneme.

Trubetzkoy clearly takes 'alternation' in a narrow sense that *ex-cludes* automatic changes (22):

> Es muß besonders betont werden, daß weder in Fällen wie rìbă :
> rĭpkă, noch in solchen, wie rèžŭ : reš für das russische Sprachbe-
> wußtsein eine Alternation von stimmhaften und stimmlosen Konsonanten
> besteht. Psychologisch handelt es sich hier vielmehr um den Wechsel
> eines stimmhaften Konsonanten mit einem hinsichtlich der Stimmbe-
> teiligung neutralen.

This point involves the notions of "neutralization" and the "archi-phoneme" introduced by R. Jakobson (1929:8ff), according to which, for example, the opposition of voicing linking Russian p and b is neutralized except before vowels and sonorants (the latter taken to include v), so that in these positions neither consonant occurs, but rather the archi-phoneme P, which possesses all the features common to both p and b. Neu-tralization itself is a phonological phenomenon but often has morpholog-ical consequences, as in Trubetzkoy's example above, where *rib-* and *riP-* are phonologically different but morphologically identical. A. Martinet (1936:56) takes the term 'alternation' to include such cases and stresses that they must be distinguished from those where neutralization is with-out morphological consequences.

In discussing Russian accentuation Trubetzkoy draws a distinction between "*rationalisierte* (sinnvolle)" and "*irrationale* (sinnlose)" alter-nations (1934:34-35). The former constitute an integral part of the gram-matical system (like English *pérmit* : *permít*) while the latter have no definable morphological function; but in Russian the categories overlap and are difficult to separate in practice (35).

After having defined the *Morphonem* Trubetzkoy makes no real use of it as a linguistic unit, however. It is not, for example, reflected in a morphonological—as opposed to phonological—system of transcription. The notion of the *Morphonem* was reduced (in the technical sense) to that of alternation, but the difficulty of treating all morphophonemic phenomena in terms of alternations rather than as processes applying to morphopho-nemic units is apparent in such a case as that of the stem *pek-* which combines with the infinitive marker *-ti* to form Old Church Slavonic *peψi*[32] (1954:106; cf. 1934:81), since this occurrence of the phoneme *ψ* must then belong to two morphemes.

In discussing *Das morphonologische System* V. Čurganova (1973:224)
notes that Trubetzkoy inappropriately treats phenomena of accent alternation as involving vowel alternations (where the vowels are in fact conditioned by the accent); T. Bulygina (1964:81-82) finds that some examples
of combinatory variation actually belong with alternations. But aside
from such less significant faults, L. Ďurovič (1967) sees the work as a
departure from Trubetzkoy's stated program:

> Gegenüber der um drei Jahre früher von ihm in *TCLP*, IV, 161
> vorgelegten Auffassung hat sich Trubetzkoy hier, und zwar völlig
> programmatisch, bloß auf deren zweiten und dritten Punkt beschränkt:
> "Die Erforschung der Arten und des Umfangs der Morphemänderung bil-
> det die Hauptaufgabe der russischen Morphonologie"; es ist also
> nicht die Aufgabe nur dieses Buches, sondern der russischen Morpho-
> nologie überhaupt. Die Erforschung der phonematischen Struktur der
> russischen Morpheme—was nach *TCLP*, IV, 161 die erste (und nach Pro-
> jet sogar die einzige) Aufgabe der Morphonologie ist—fiel aus.
> [558]

> Tatsächlich, die Termini 'Alternation', 'Alternationspaar', 'Wech-
> selreihe', 'Ablautsreihe', 'Ablautspaar' und 'Morphonem' werden
> promiscue für dieselben Sachen gebraucht und es gibt ganze Kapiteln,
> in denen der Terminus 'Morphonem' gar nicht vorkommt.
>   Der Begriff 'Morphonem' ist also in *TCLP*, IV, 2 offensichtlich
> überflüssig. [560]

Ďurovič goes on to observe (560-61) that Trubetzkoy's *Grundzüge der
Phonologie* (1939) makes use of neither the *Morphonem* nor *Morphonologie*;
the division of *Wort- und Morphemphonologie* is dropped, and phonology is
expanded so as to include the phonological structure of morphemes (cf.
Trubetzkoy 1939:225) and *kombinatorische Morphemveränderungen*. Ďurovič
draws the implications of these changes (561):

> Aus dem gesagten ist es ersichtlich, daß Trubetzkoy in *Grund-
> zügen* . . . seine früheren Ansichten wesentlich revidierte. Aus
> seinen veröffentlichten Werken kann man nicht feststellen, welche
> Einstellung er zu den Begriffen 'Morphonologie' und 'Morphonem' in
> seinen letzten Lebensjahren hatte. Entweder hat er sie völlig auf-
> gegeben (davon würde das Schweigen in den *Grundzügen* . . . zeugen),
> oder hat er sie für die Lehre von den freien Morphemveränderungen
> anheimgestellt. Für die zweite Alternative spricht zunächst die Er-
> wähnung der Herausgeber in dem Vorwort zu *TCLP*, VII, daß Trubetzkoy
> in dem zweiten Teil der *Grundzügen* . . . auch ein Kapitel über Mor-
> phonologie einfügen wollte.

Trubetzkoy's final views remain unclear to us. But whether he abandoned or simply narrowed his theory of morphonology, the changes seem to be consonant with the criticism of morphonology from other European linguists; this criticism will be the focus of attention in Chapter IV, "European Structuralism after Trubetzkoy".

CHAPTER III

AMERICAN LINGUISTICS THROUGH BLOOMFIELD

William Dwight Whitney

One might expect to find a significant contribution to the general understanding of alternations and morphophonemics in the works of the eminent American Sanskritist William Dwight Whitney (1827-94). A ground for this expectation is to be seen in this observation of his (1884:27ᶜ

> The character of the Hindu grammatical science was, as is usu-
> al in such cases, determined by the character of its subject. The
> Sanskrit is above all things an analyzable language, one admitting
> of the easy and distinct separation of ending from stem, and of de-
> rivative suffix from primitive word, back to the ultimate attain-
> able elements, the so-called roots. Accordingly, in its perfected
> form (for all the preparatory stages are unknown to us), the Hindu
> grammar offers us an established body of roots, with rules for
> their conversion into stems and for the inflection of the latter,
> and also for the accompanying phonetic changes—this last involving
> and resting upon a phonetic science of extraordinary merit.

But Whitney failed to see the implications of Hindu grammatical science for a general theory of language. He considered linguistics to be a
purely modern science (1875:4-5) and one with an exclusively historical
basis (312):

> As linguistics is a historical science, so its evidences are
> historical, and its methods of proof of the same character.

Whitney's preoccupation with language history led him utterly to
confuse the diachronic and synchronic processes of language, e.g. (1867:
92):

> The conversion of a surd letter into its corresponding sonant,
> or of a sonant into surd, is abundantly illustrated in the history
> of every language. Our own plural sign, *s*, is pronounced as *s* only
> when it follows another surd consonant, as in *plants, cakes;* after
> a sonant consonant or a vowel, it becomes *z*, as in *eyes, pins, pegs.*

In the same paragraph he goes on to discuss the replacement of the
form *loveth* with *loves* in English as a change of the same nature (93).
M. Silverstein (1971:xxi) characterizes the basic shortcoming of Whitney's approach to alternation:

> It becomes clear, however, that in Whitney's case, as in the
> cases of later writers, like Franz Boas and Sapir in certain phases,
> the phonological 'euphony,' the dynamic alternations of shape in
> elements of a language in different constructions, is primarily a
> reflection of historical processes, the geological evidence, so to
> speak, of what must have gone on through time. We miss a clear idea
> of the independent systemic status of such alternations.

Whitney states that his objective is to present the Sanskrit language as it is found in Sanskrit literature rather than according to the
prescriptions of the Hindu grammarians (1884:292; 1889:v, xiv). He makes
it quite clear that he does not regard Pāṇini's description as a model
(1884:280):

> Its form of presentation is of the strangest: a miracle of ingenu-
> ity, but of perverse and wasted ingenuity. The only object aimed at
> in it is brevity, at the sacrifice of everything else—of order, of
> clearness, of even intelligibility except by the aid of keys and
> commentaries and lists of words, which then are furnished in profu-
> sion.

Whitney was greatly concerned with statistical analysis and the at-
testation of actual forms. In a passage that might remind one of criticism of transformational grammar,[1] this emphasis leads him to find fault
in the formalistic character of rules that produce forms not actually
used (1884:280):

> Since there is nothing to show how far the application of a rule
> reaches, there are provided treatises of laws of interpretation to
> be applied to them; but there is a residual rule underlying and de-
> termining the whole: that both the grammar and the laws of interpre-
> tation must be so construed as to yield good and acceptable forms,
> and not otherwise—and this implies (if that were needed) a condem-
> nation of the whole mode of presentation of the system as a failure.

But in accordance with Whitney's own observation it was inevitable
that the character of the language itself would influence the structure
of his *Sanskrit Grammar*, which contains 54 pages on "Rules of Euphonic
Combination". Whitney makes the significant observation that a knowledge
of the rules of combination is necessary not only for an active command
of the language but in order to be able to read it at all (1889:34-35);
this factor undoubtedly contributes to the special position of morphophonemics in Sanskrit grammar.

Whitney's scattered remarks on alternation are of historical interest in a discussion of morphophonemics, but they provided no real basis
for later study. It was the investigation of native American languages
in the nineteenth century and earlier by missionaries and technically un-
trained observers,[2] rather than the neogrammarian scholarship of Whitney,
that provided a point of departure for Boas, the next of the four great
American linguists discussed in this chapter.

Franz Boas

The early interest of Franz Boas (1858-1942) in the methodological
problems of overdifferentiation and underdifferentiation in the percep-
tion of foreign speech sounds, as reflected in his "On Alternating
Sounds" (1889) should—and in fact may—have led him to the phonemic
principle. But the main lesson he drew from this study was that earlier
practice in transcription had been largely faulty, and that accurate phonetic transcription was the proper departure point for scientific study
of America's native languages. His fear of phonetic inaccuracy is reflected in the very narrow transcription found in most of his grammars and
in many works produced under his guidance. The discrepancy between Boas's
theory and practice may be comparable to that of Bloomfield, who taught
the ideas of phonemics but usually transcribed morphophonemically. Boas's
grammatical writings do not reflect the later distinction between subphonemic variation and automatic (morphophonemic) alternation.

In his *Handbook of American Indian Languages* (1911) Boas follows tradition in speaking of "laws of euphony" (290ff, 431ff), which govern the combination of sounds and may be progressive, regressive, or recip- rocal in nature (431). He identifies these laws with the sandhi of San- skrit grammar (79-80). In other places he uses the expression 'phonetic law' (566ff) or 'phonetic change' (884ff). Unfortunately, sound shifts, sound correspondences between dialects, alternations, and—probably— subphonemic variation are all presented together.

But Boas clearly distinguishes nonautomatic changes, which he calls "etymological" (436), from other types:

> While the rule just described is founded entirely on the pho- netic influence of the stem element upon its suffix, we also have a class of phonetic changes which are due to etymological causes, and can not be brought entirely under phonetic rules. . . . Thus the compound of the stem $q\bar{a}s$- TO WALK, and the suffix -$x^{\epsilon}\bar{\imath}d$ TO BE- GIN, would result in the phonetically admissable combination $q\bar{a}sx^{\epsilon}\bar{\imath}d$, which we find in a word like $^{\epsilon}w\bar{a}lasx\hat{e}'$ LYNX. Nevertheless, the resulting form is $q\bar{a}s^{\epsilon}\bar{\imath}d$. The elision of the initial sound of the suffix is therefore not entirely due to phonetic causes, and must be treated in detail in a discussion of the suffixes. [1911: 433]

> Only the first two of these laws are purely phonetic, while the others are restricted to certain grammatical forms. [1911:566]

And we can infer that Boas makes another distinction in changes de- pending on whether or not they correspond to a difference in meaning (1917:20):

> The significance of the stem is modified by internal changes,[3] which affect pitch and quality of the stem-vowel, but which in some cases extend farther, certain consonants being either added or omit- ted.

The principle of base forms is unmistakably to be seen in the fol- lowing passage (1911:291):

> Before g and k, terminal sonants become surds . . ..
> Before t and vowels, the sound remains a sonant . . ..
> The fact that some terminal sounds always remain surd shows that in the cases of alternation[4] of surd and sonant the latter must be considered the stem consonant.

A technique found in Boas's Tlingit study is entirely comparable to Bloomfield's use of morphophonemic symbols: in his notation he distingui-

shes two sounds that are alike in pronunciation "because the behavior of
the two sounds is quite different" (1917:10); the following passage shows
that this difference of behavior involves alternation (15).

The same work contains a section on "Phonetic Processes" that once
again illustrates the special care with which Boas describes nonautomatic
changes (16):

> The vowel *u*, the semi-vowel *w*, and all labialized palatal and
> velar *k*-sounds, bring about the labialization of many *k*-sounds im-
> mediately following them. . . . This rule applies only to certain
> suffixes and prefixes. It does not imply that *k*-sounds of the stem,
> when following a *u*, *w*, or a labialized *k*-sound are assimilated
> . . ..
> Labialized *k*-sounds may also follow other vowels.

His late *Dakota Grammar* and the posthumous *Kwakiutl Grammar* give a
lucid handling of alternations (1941:6-22; 1947:211-19) but make no theoretical contribution on the subject and in any case fall in a later period.

Edward Sapir

The lack of a general treatise on alternation from Boas is in part
compensated for by the book *Language* (1921) written by his student Edward Sapir (1884-1939). Unfortunately, the book does not develop as systematic a terminology as Bloomfield's *Language* (1933); the "method of
postulates" certainly is foreign to its style. But it is not, nor was it
intended to be, a technical work on the scale of Bloomfield's, so that
its less rigorous terminology may or may not be a reflection of Sapir's
theory itself.

Nevertheless, obviously following Boas's teaching, Sapir presents a
classification that opposes "external, mechanical" changes, with no functional significance, to "internal changes", which are grammatical processes (1921:62):

> It is important to bear in mind that a linguistic phenomenon
> cannot be looked upon as illustrating a definite "process" unless
> it has an inherent functional value. The consonantal change in En-
> glish, for instance, of *book-s* and *bag-s* (*s* in the former, *z* in the

latter) is of no functional significance. It is a purely external,
mechanical change induced by the presence of a preceding voiceless
consonant, *k*, in the former case, of a voiced consonant, *g*, in the
latter. This mechanical alternation is objectively the same as that
between the noun *house* and the verb *to house*. In the latter case,
however, it has an important grammatical function, that of trans-
forming a noun into a verb. The two alternations belong, then, to
entirely different psychological categories. Only the latter is a
true illustration of consonantal modification as a grammatical process.

This passage should make it clear that Boas's "internal change" is
not confined to *within* words or morphemes but may include changes at
morpheme boundaries and necessarily involves a grammatical function.
Sapir goes on to illustrate internal change with examples from Hebrew
and other languages (73-76). He shows a keen appreciation for the subtle
interaction of phonetic and grammatical processes, and for how the former, through analogy and sound change, can be replaced by the latter (75,
189-91).

In his early *Takelma* (1922:59)[5] Sapir notes that both external and
internal changes may result in homonyms. In practice he works with base
forms and rules of combination, and much later he actually speaks of an
"underlying phonologic configuration" (1949:57) as both a descriptive
device and a psychological reality.[6]

Sapir presents some of his most interesting remarks on alternation
in his two famous papers, "Sound Patterns in Language" (1925) and "The
Psychological Reality of Phonemes" (1933).[7] In the following passage
from the earlier work his views approach those of the Prague Linguistics
Circle (1949:42):

> The fact that in English we have morphological alternations
> like *wife* : *wives*, *sheath* : *to sheathe*, *breath* : *to breathe*, *mouse* :
> *mouse*, helps to give the sounds *f*, *θ*, *s* an intuitive pattern rela-
> tion to their voiced correlates *v*, *ð*, *z* which is specifically dif-
> ferent from the theoretically analogous relation *p*, *t*, *k* : *b*, *d*, *g*;
> in English, *f* is nearer to *v* than *p* is to *b*, but in German this cer-
> tainly is not true.

This line of thinking is pushed further in the later paper, where
Sapir claims that "the word *led* . . . is felt as having a vowel which
has been deflected from the vowel of *lead* [i.e. the verb] and is there-

fore not psychologically homonymous with the word for a metal, *lead*, in
which the vowel is felt to be primary, not deflected . . ." (1949:52).
In effect he argues that phonetically identical forms may require different phonemic—or, depending on one's viewpoint, morphophonemic—representations. Sapir was drawn to the new theory of morphophonemics, and
in one of his last works (1938) he uses the term 'morphophonemic' re-
peatedly (1949:227-29).[8] 'Alternation' also appears in a technical sense
and apparently with a narrow usage that is diametrically opposed to that
of Trubetzkoy: "These alternations, if present, could not easily develop
systematic morphophonemic significance . . .." (1949:238).

But the problem with Sapir is that we have so little material from
him on the problem of alternation and morphophonemics.[9] His death in
1939 was early, and he never consolidated his views into a theory of
this phenomenon. Early American linguistics suffered from its unfamili-
arity with the Kazan School's theory of alternation, and no American
provided a discussion of comparable value before Leònard Bloomfield
(1887-1949).

Leonard Bloomfield

Bloomfield's *An Introduction to the Study of Language* takes account
of the phonemic principle (1914:54):

> Each language, or better, each dialect distinguishes only a
> limited number of places of articulation, and in each place only a
> limited number of manners of articulation, and any variations from
> these are never significant.

However, such variation, termed 'automatic sound-variation' (55) is
grouped together with sandhi phenomena (102, 128) and the alternation
shown by the regular English plural ending (136); it contrasts with 'morphological sound-variation' (152, 156), which has grammatical significance. Thus, the distinction Bloomfield makes is essentially the same as
that of Boas and Sapir between 'external' and 'internal' changes. No reference is made to the works of Saussure or Baudouin de Courtenay although
numerous other linguists are mentioned.

Bloomfield's grammar of Tagalog presents a striking foreshadowing of his later theoretical views (1917:§332):

> Other modifications besides affixation, 'doubling', and redu-
> plication affecting the meaning are *shifting of the accent* toward
> the end of the word, and the use of *secondary accents*.
> Modifications not affecting the meaning, but merely accompany-
> ing those already named, are *sound-variation* and *retraction of the
> accent* toward the beginning of the word.
> The same morphologic elements may be variously distributed; it
> is most convenient and corresponds most nearly to the speech-feeling
> to describe these differences as though they were due to different
> successions in which the modifications are applied: sumù-súlat is
> súlat reduplicated and with the infix -um-; but (nag-)tùtu-mirà is
> tirà with infix -um-, then reduplicated (plus prefix nag-).
> The part of a word to which a modification is (in this sense)
> said to be added will be called the *underlying word* (or phrase)
> . . ..

Bloomfield's notions of sequential derivation and "underlying" elements are seen here, but one must note that the latter term is used as
in his *Language*, as discussed below. And the principle of ordering, while
important for Tagalog, is implicit in the work and does not appear as an
overt feature of its structure, as it does in "Menomini Morphophonemics".[10]
The subsequent passages contain a full description of the phonemic structure of morphemes (§333) and the distribution of alternations (§334) together with the account of the alternations themselves. Bloomfield actually speaks of sounds "alternating" with others (§§16-20), but his approach is based on rules of combination. No general classification of alternations emerges from the work.

Nor can one find such a classification in his "Notes on the Fox Language" (1925), which closely follows the framework of Sanskrit grammar.
Excellent in technique, the work seems theoretically noncommittal in comparison with the earlier Tagalog study. It is important, however, for its
remarks on productivity, which are reflected in the description itself
(1925:§13):

> When morphologic elements come together within a word, they are
> subject to variations which differ from those of external sandhi.
> There is great irregularity, because words are kept which embody
> some old law of internal combination that is no longer active and is
> violated in newer formations. It is therefore important to distin-

guish between habits of combination which are carried out in the
actual language and mere traces of older habits (irregularities).

"A Set of Postulates for the Science of Language" (1926) finally
provides a general discussion of alternations. Bloomfield's classification[11] includes the following distinctions:

(1) The alternation of a phoneme "with another phoneme according to
accompanying phonemes" (§39) is *phonetic*, as opposed to the *formal*
alternation of a form in a construction "with another form according
to accompanying forms" (§41).
(2) Formal alternations are *automatic* if "determined by the phonemes
of the accompanying forms" (§45) and otherwise are *grammatical* (§47).
(3) Members of a grammatically determined alternation are *regular*
if they predominate in number and otherwise are *irregular* (§48).

The influence of Sanskrit grammar is to be seen in Bloomfield's examples, but one also notes with particular interest his reference to
Baudouin's *Versuch*.

Language (1933) shows the development of its author's thoughts on
alternation since the "Postulates". In §13.4 two terms are defined differently than in the earlier work:

(1) An alternation is *phonetic* if the difference between its members
"can be described in terms of phonetic modification" and otherwise
is *suppletive* (cf. §13.7; 1926:§49).
(2) An alternation is *regular* if the distribution of alternants "is
regulated according to a linguistically recognizable characteristic
of the accompanying forms".

Several terms are either clarified or introduced:

(3) An *underlying form*, equivalent to an *underlying word* (cf. §13.9),
is the free form in a derived secondary word (the latter being a
word which contains, but is not identical to, a single free form).
e.g. *boy* in *boyish*, *old maid* in *old-maidish*, *glass* in *glasses*, and
land in *landed* (§13.3-4). 'Derivation' is taken here to include inflection.
(4) A *basis* (cf. §13.7) or *basic form* is the member of an alternation that has the wider or widest "range", i.e. that is least limi-
ted in its distribution; other members of the alternation are char-
acterized in terms of modifications of this form (§10.4).

The reader will note that the current general usage of 'underlying'
and 'basic' differs from that found here. This may have resulted from a

shift of emphasis in reading passages where Bloomfield speaks of "setting up" an "artificial underlying" or a "theoretical basic" form (§13. 9). The terms 'artificial' and 'theoretical' in these passages are now often understood as having been used by Bloomfield to characterize "underlying" or "basic" forms in general; but this veers from the original intent, for he clearly means to oppose *these* basic or underlying forms to those that are pronounced without phonetic modifications from the shape of their morphological representations.[12]

Parallel to the above distinction is Bloomfield's emphasis that the order of statements specifying successive modifications of morphological elements to arrive at pronounced forms is "purely descriptive", and that the speaker does not in fact pass through such successive steps (§13.6):

> The terms "before, after, first, then," and so on, in such statements, tell the *descriptive order*. The actual sequence of constituents, and their structural order (§13.3) are a part of the language, but the descriptive order of grammatical features is a fiction and results simply from our method of describing the forms; it goes without saying, for instance, that the speaker who says *knives*, does not "first" replace [f] by [v] and "then" add [-z], but merely utters a form (*knives*) which in certain features differs from a certain other form (namely, *knife*).

It is important to note that it is simplicity of description that justifies the use of such artificial devices (§13.9):

> We have seen that when forms are partially similar, there may be a question as to which one we had better take as the underlying form, and that the structure of the language may decide this question for us, since, taking it one way, we get an unduly complicated description, and, taking it the other way, a relatively simple one. This same consideration often leads us to *set up* an artificial underlying form.

An equally fundamental point in the above passage is that the use of theoretical forms and descriptive order was not *arbitrary* for Bloomfield. But he was suspicious of such devices and did not fully appreciate their value, kept close to units he considered to be "actual", and made no use of such terms as 'morphophonemics' and 'morphophoneme'.

Both terms, however, are highlighted in his "Menomini Morphophonemics" (1939), where he defines "internal sandhi or morphophonemics" as

the variation of morphological elements as they enter into different combinations (§2); it is to be distinguished from "morpholexical variation",
which is irregular, yet still involves phonetic modification rather than
suppletion (§3).

Bloomfield again speaks of "theoretical basic forms" and "ordered"
rules, but the former may now be set up merely to bar application of a
rule (§16), while the rules themselves are developed into a system of
complexity not suggested in *Language*. The term 'morphophoneme' is applied
to the units that make up the theoretical basic forms, but, uncharacter-
istically, no definition is provided for the unit.

In the best known paragraph of the paper, Bloomfield confronts the
parallels between historical and morphophonemic description but offers
no explanation (§4):

> The process of description leads us to set up each morphologi-
> cal element in a theoretical *basic* form, and then to state the de-
> viations from this basic form which appear when the element is com-
> bined with other elements. If one starts with the basic forms and
> applies our statements (§§10 and following) in the order in which
> we give them, one will arrive finally at forms of words as they are
> actually spoken. Our basic forms are not ancient forms, say of the
> Proto-Algonquian parent language, and our statements of internal
> sandhi are not historical but descriptive, and appear in a purely
> *descriptive order*. However, our basic forms do bear some resemblance
> to those which would be set up for a description of Proto-Algonquian,
> some of our statements of alternation (namely, those in §§10 to 18)
> resemble those which would appear in a description of Proto-Algon-
> quian, and the rest (§§19 and following), as to content and order,
> approximate the historical development to present-day Menomini.

The above passage shows again that the choice of theoretical basic
forms is not *arbitrary*, for mention of the parallel would in that case
be gratuitous. Bloomfield saw basic forms, like alternations, as presenting problems arising directly from primary data:

> You tell about the reduced forms, but not about the basic
> forms. These are plain enough when there is an alternation, and it
> is our job to find them. [Bloomfield (1970:373) to Hockett in 1938]

In contrast, it was the question of notation and arrangement of information in a description that was to a certain extent arbitrary for
him in that it could be answered by the particular aims of linguists:

> Standard German has non-final bdgzv and ptksf, but in final position only the latter set. In morphology former in word-final ∿ [is replaced in alternation by] latter: rund-e : runt, cf. bunt-e : bunt. (Against Twaddell, if I understand him right, we identify medial and final ptksf.) Now, these are the facts which the language gives us—the things the speakers do. I don't understand such questions as "*Is* a final p the same phoneme as a medial p or as a medial b or a third phoneme?" The only question I can see is a choice that is entirely in our hands: we can describe the facts in various ways. [Bloomfield (1970:374) to Hockett in 1939]

"Menomini Morphophonemics" gives a clear example of Bloomfield's technique in §13.[13] The sound *n* alternates with *s* before certain palatal sounds. But some instances of *n* belong to no alternation; these are represented by the morphophoneme *N* in transcription to distinguish them from the others, to which the rule applies. This contrasts with his handling of essentially the same alternation in "Notes on the Fox Language" (§22), where the cases of nonalternating *n*, being relatively few, are simply listed.

Bloomfield's debt to Pāṇini is evident throughout his grammatical writings, and his great respect for the latter is directly expressed in *Language* (1933:11), "On Some Rules of Pāṇini" (1927), and "Review of Liebich" (1929). The last work contains the following passages:

> The descriptive grammar of Sanskrit, which Pāṇini brought to its highest perfection, is one of the greatest monuments of human intelligence and (what concerns us more) an indispensable model for the description of languages. The only achievement in our field which can take rank with it is the historical linguistics of the nineteenth century, and this, indeed, owed its origin largely to Europe's acquaintance with the Indian grammar. [268]

> Indo-European comparative grammar had (and has) at its service only one complete description of a language, the grammar of Pāṇini. For all other Indo-European languages it had only the traditional grammars of Greek and Latin, wofully incomplete and unsystematic. [270]

> For no language of the past have we a record comparable to Pāṇini's record of his mother-tongue, nor is it likely that any language spoken today will be so perfectly recorded. [274]

Special criticism is directed at some of Whitney's disparaging remarks (268-69):

Indian grammar has been undervalued and neglected by many linguists, especially in America. . . . Consequently, the European saw
in classical texts a primary document, in the grammar a secondary
one and unreliable at that. This was Whitney's view, to which he
gave unfortunate expression. We now know that this view was the reverse of the truth.

The insistence that Pāṇini's work be taken as a "model" must be
read literally; Bloomfield's view of language and his method of description derive in large measure from those of the ancient linguist. But
even Bloomfield has reservations about the use of rule-ordering and its
effect on the arrangement of subject-matter (271-72):

A third method of abbreviation is less happy. Although the basic arrangement of Pāṇini's treatise was relevant to the subject-
matter, he subordinated this logical order to a requirement of con-
ciseness: every rule is so placed that as many as possible of its
words can be replaced by ditto marks because they repeat words of
the preceding rule. For this purpose so many rules are torn from
their natural place that the basic structure of the grammar is to a
large extent obscured. . . .

A fourth and even more unfortunate means of compression pre-
vents our rearranging the rules. Even if one restores the words
that have been replaced by imaginary ditto marks, one cannot rear-
range the rules in natural order, because the position of a rule is
one of the features which determines its validity (with relation to
apparently conflicting rules) and its order of application (with relation to other rules that apply to the same form). Other features
also, such as the more or less specific character of its wording,
have to be considered in deciding whether a rule is applicable and
in what relative order.

This last passage undoubtedly is a reflection of Bloomfield's general reticence on the issue of ordered rules in morphophonemics.

Although it is a digression, one might pause here to wonder about
the circumstances that attended Bloomfield's decision to submit "Menomini
Morphophonemics" as his invited contribution to the memorial volume of
Travaux du Cercle linguistique de Prague for Trubetzkoy, who died in 1938.
The two scholars studied together in 1913 in Leipzig,[14] and each must
have been aware of the work of the other. Yet Trubetzkoy's only mention
of Bloomfield in his *Grundzüge der Phonologie* is a brief reference to
the latter's "Notes";[15] Bloomfield does no more than acknowledge the existence of *TCLP* in his *Language*.

It seems reasonable to conclude that Bloomfield's choice of the
title "Menomini Morphophonemics" for his paper was explicitly intended
to honor Trubetzkoy and recognize his theoretical contributions. But
neither this nor Bloomfield's earlier works give a picture of the position of morphophonemics within his own framework.[16]

Whatever further development Bloomfield's ideas may have taken is
unclear. "On Describing Inflection" (1945), written as a response to a
complicated description of French verb morphophonemics by G. Trager
(1944), employs morphophonemic "effect" symbols and consists of an introduction and general statement plus a list of 58 Paninian statements
to cover exceptions. The introduction is notable for its assertion that
"A less rigorous statement may be more useful even for scientific purposes" (1945:8; also 1970:439). The terms 'morphophoneme' and 'morphophonemics' do not appear, however, and Bloomfield wrote no more on the
subject before his death in 1949.[17]

The posthumously published *Eastern Ojibwa* and *The Menomini Language*
continue to practice the technique of morphophonemics, and the ·second
work is unquestionably Bloomfield's finest piece of grammatical writing.
But they pull away from the theoretical questions raised earlier and
speak only of "special symbols" rather than "morphophonemes" (1962:80).

:: :: ::

From the period surveyed thus far (in Chapters I-III) it is evident
that the inception of morphophonemic theory was coupled with the distinction of sounds as against phonemes, on the one hand, and phonemes as
against morphophonemes, on the other. Great progress came early, especially in the unjustly neglected works of Baudouin and Kruszewski, but
this was largely overshadowed by the dominant concern with historical
studies in linguistics. By the end of the period, the two outstanding
figures that had emerged were Trubetzkoy and Bloomfield.

Bloomfield's greatest merit lies in the scope and rigor of his theory, with its subtle distinctions and carefully constructed terminology.
His ordered rules handle phenomena outside the limits of Trubetzkoy's

theory, and his "special symbols" or morphophonemic diacritics are an important device that still is a focus of theoretical debate.

Trubetzkoy, however, gives a unified view of the phenomena Bloomfield treats separately and thus surpasses the latter in his conception of morphonology as "the study of the morphological utilization of the phonological means of a language". Likewise, his recognition of phonological distinctive features allows him to show parallelisms that escape Bloomfield's treatment.

Neither linguists makes the distinction reflected in the later term 'allomorph'; Bloomfield shows this in his equivocal (apparently, technical and nontechnical) use of the term 'form'.[18] Another error is Bloomfield's failure consistently to distinguish "regular" from "productive" alternations.[19]

Both linguists mirror the nonlinguistic issues of their times. Trubetzkoy frames his definitions in terms of "consciousness" and "ideas", while Bloomfield is preoccupied with separating "real" and "actual" entities from those he considers "fictitious" or "theoretical". Unprejudiced reading, however, shows that this does not distract in substance from the studies of either.

The work of Trubetzkoy and Bloomfield was complementary, and taken together it formed the basis for subsequent investigation of morphophonemics.

CHAPTER IV

EUROPEAN STRUCTURALISM AFTER TRUBETZKOY

Trubetzkoy's theory of morphonology quickly attracted the attention
of other European linguists. Reaction was largely skeptical, however,
and this skepticism was directed mainly toward the view that morphonology
was an area of investigation *distinct* from those areas which had already
been recognized. Ďurovič (1967:556) states the issue:

> Zum Unterschied von anderen traditionsmäßig beständigen und
> zweifellosen linguistischen Disziplinen, muß man sich im Zusammen-
> hang mit der Morphonologie eine principielle Frage stellen: Hat die
> Morphonologie als selbständige linguistische Disziplin, neben der
> Phonologie und Morphologie, einen Zweck? Wenn ja, was ist dann ihr
> Gegenstand?

Dutch linguists were among the first to respond directly to this
question in articles. N. Van Wijk (1934) agrees that the material Trubetzkoy includes within morphonology is important but rejects the new
terminology and the claim (in Trubetzkoy 1931) that earlier linguists,
especially scholars in Indo-European, had ignored the area; he calls
special attention to the discussion of alternation in Meillet's *Introduction* and concludes that Trubetzkoy's proposals constitute no substan-
tial advance. One should also note Van Wijk's insistence that morphonology not be understood as a part of phonology (1934:115):

> Another question is whether the new term "morphonology" was
> necessary. Meillet got along without such terminological fads; is
> that no longer possible in our day? To be sure, "morphophoneme" is
> not a badly constructed compound . . ., but wasn't a term like "pho-
> neme alternation" good? For that matter, "morphonology" seems even
> worse to me. For "the study of morphonemes" one could have used

"morphoneme-ology". Now, I realize that "morphonology" was manufactured on the analogy of the pair "phoneme" : "phonology" with "morphoneme", but I still consider the term badly chosen. Whenever "phonology" stands beside "morphonology", then our speech feeling takes this second term as a compound built from the first, and that leads to misunderstanding, as if "mor-phonology" were a sort of phonology. Whenever such—in my judgment—monstrous terms exist by tradition, then I accept them without objection, but why are they made now?

Van Wijk's book *Phonologie* (1939) devotes a chapter (126-31) to "The So-called Morphonology". The terms 'morphoneme' and 'morphonology' are both rejected, and Van Wijk again claims that 'alternation' as used by Meillet is adequate to discuss all the aspects of Trubetzkoy's morphonology. He also holds that morphonology—if it is to be recognized at all—is a division of morphology (1939:126):

> Morphonology is "die Erforschung der morphologischen Ausnützung der phonologischen Mittel einer Sprache". It follows from this definition that morphonology belongs more properly in morphology than in phonology.

J. Kats's analysis of a Dutch dialect (1939) is based on Trubetzkoy 1934 and Van Ginneken 1934 and is noteworthy as one of the very few applications of morphonological theory as Trubetzkoy conceived it.[1] But other Dutch linguists generally adopted the position of Van Wijk. A. Weijnen notes (1944:205) that a disadvantage of the term 'morphoneme' arose through its conflicting usage by different linguists:

> Actually, the term 'morphoneme' or 'morphophoneme' isn't bad, but it is used in three different senses. H. Ułaszyn, who invented it, understood it as "ein Phonema in semasiologisch-morphologischer Funktion", which thus actually makes for little difference from the sense of 'phoneme'. Van Ginneken has never defined the word but seems to mean by it approximately: a phoneme, *insofar as* it occurs in endings or affixes. . . . And thirdly, we have Trubetzkoy's definition . . ..

Morphonology naturally received special attention within the Prague Circle, where the notion had originated. But discussion was confined to a criticism of principles, and no further applications of it are to be seen in descriptive works. J. Vachek (1961:66) includes 'morphoneme' among "les termes qui ont vieilli au cours de l'évolution ou bien ceux qui ont été abandonées",[2] and Ďurovič (1967:561) flatly states that "andere Mitglieder der Prager Schule, Trubetzkoys Zeitgenossen, haben seine Idee der Morphonologie offensichtlich nicht angenommen".

The basic objection that developed within the Prague Circle was that morphonology had no distinct domain of its own. The line of argumentation was that *kombinatorische Morphemveränderung* was essentially a matter of neutralization and consequently belonged to phonology, while *freie Morphemveränderung* served a morphological (i.e. significant) function and therefore was the concern of morphology.

The principle of neutralization—introduced, like morphonology, by the Prague Circle—was rejected by most American linguists of the 1940's. Hockett (1942a:§7.2), for example, asserts that a "simple statement of distribution . . . gives the facts without any complications; any talk of neutralization or archiphonemes confuses the facts without adding anything." On the other hand, neutralization was readily accepted by the Prague Circle. Martinet criticizes both American morphophonemics and Trubetzkoy's morphonology for failing to treat *kombinatorische Morphemveränderungen* within phonology:

> A fairly common methodological mistake with beginners consists in confusing phonemic and morphological alternations. The use of the term 'morphophonemics' (or 'morphonology') as applied to the latter, does not help to clarify matters, as it suggests that the study of such alternations is a chapter, or at least an annex of phonemics proper. Using the concept of neutralization for stressing the peculiar nature of phonemic alternations has proved to be instrumental in preventing the confusion, but . . . English-speaking phonemicists usually fail to appreciate the practical value of that concept. [1949b:19]

> La façon dont Trubetzkoy organise son ouvrage va, de son côté, contribuer à estomper les différences fondamentales entre phonologie et morphonologie. Il distingue bien entre les modifications combinatoires (*kombinatorische Morphemveränderung*) et les modifications qui ne sont pas sous la dépendance du contexte phonique (*freie Morphemveränderung*) les seules qu'il désigne comme des alternances (*Alternationen*). Mais il néglige certaines précautions indispensables: les modifications combinatoires correspondent normalement à des neutralisations (type *ryba/rybka*, /rîba/ ∿ /rîPka/) et on aurait dû nous rappeler expressément qu'elles n'entraient pas dans le cadre de la morphonologie, mais dans celui de la phonologie. [1965:18]

Just the opposite criticism is made by Harris (1941b:349), however, who claims that Trubetzkoy's *Grundzüge* groups together all neutralizations without regard for their morphological consequences:

> The value of Trubetzkoy's discussion is limited by the fact that he groups together all neutralizations, both those which would be eliminated in morphophonemic formulae (in cases where the neutralized and contrasted positions of a phoneme occur in two forms of the same morpheme) as well as those which constitute the purely phonemic positional limitations of the phoneme in questions (where no morpheme could have it in both neutralized and contrasted positions).

Hockett later modified his view toward neutralization. His only objection is "that the notion of neutralization can handle only some of the distributional limitations in a language" (1951;337), but he decides that "the usual American objections to the Trubetzkoyan way of stating the situation seem rather trivial" (336). Hockett expressly states (337 fn.) that Martinet's use of the term 'neutralization' does not involve "invalid use of morphophonemic considerations on the phonemic level".

But Americans have continued to speak seldom in terms of neutralization, and a fundamental split with Europeans on the issue is evident. Much of the American opposition rested on the "once a phoneme—always a phoneme" doctrine that forbids complete overlapping and requires that a given sound always be phonemically transcribed the same way under the same conditions.[3] This requirement implies that *kombinatorische Morphemveränderung* involves the alternation of phonemically distinct forms even when it rests on distributional limitations in phonology; the attempt to handle such alternation as a purely phonological phenomenon was then seen as a mixing of grammar with phonology. European linguists, however, have always rejected the requirement and its consequences. C. E. Bazell is typical in maintaining that neutralization phenomena belong properly to the domain of phonology (1956:29-30):

> Many neutralizations are positively relevant to morphological description, i.e. the failure to take them into account on the phonological level leads either to a complication of morphological description or else to an otherwise superfluous "morphophonemics" designed to bridge the gap between phoneme and morpheme. . . . It suf-

fices to state that the feature "voice" is suppressed in word-final position (Russian, German, Turkish), and nothing further remains to be added when one passes from phonemics to morphemics.

So, Trubetzkoy's conception of morphonology was attacked from one side by the relegation of *kombinatorische Morphemveränderung* to phonology. But then from the opposite direction came another objection: that *freie Morphemveränderung*—alternation in the strict sense—essentially belonged to morphology. Ďurovič (1967:558) states the position concisely:

> Die Alternationen sind ein Bestandteil der formellen Signalisierung der grammatischen Formen, bzw. der Wortbildungstypen und ihre Beschreibung ist deshalb ein integrierender Bestandteil der Morphologie bzw. der Lexikologie der betreffenden Sprache.

Martinet (1949a:6) criticizes morphonology as being a mistaken treatment of morphology as phonology:

> Most beginners are tempted to give a phonological status to such alternations as [$\tilde{\varepsilon}$/in] in French on account of the morphological use of them in words like *fin-fine, coquin-coquine*. Such alternations are certainly part and parcel of the French system of to-day, as is shown in the case of [$\tilde{\varepsilon}$/in] by its recent extension to words like *copain* whose popular feminine is *copine*. But this of course does not mean that they belong to the domain of phonology. It was a serious mistake on the part of Trubetzkoy to include a chapter called 'morphonology' (short for morphophonology) in his plan of phonological studies.

The same view is echoed in the short section titled 'La "morphonologie"' in Martinet's *Eléments de linguistique générale* (1960:§3.41):

> On est souvent tenté d'inclure dans la présentation de la phonologie d'une langue un examen des alternances vocaliques ou consonantiques telles que celles de *eu* et de *ou* dans *peuvent, pouvons, meurent, mourons, preuve, prouvons*, etc. ou encore les inflexions de l'allemand qu'on groupe sous le terme de *Umlaut* et qui servent pour former des pluriels comme *Bücher* ou des formes verbales comme *fällt* ou *gibt*. Cet examen, pratiqué sous le nom de morpho-(pho)nologie, est parfaitement justifié lorsqu'il vise à dégager certains automatismes comme celui qui entraîne le petit Allemand à former, à partir de *bringen, gebrungen* au lieu de *gebracht*, sur le modèle de *singen, gesungen*. Mais ceci n'a rien à voir avec la phonologie; le conditionnement de l'alternance est strictement morphologique et n'est, en aucune façon, déterminé par des facteurs phoniques. Le terme de morpho(pho)nologie, qui laisse supposer un rapport avec la phonologie, est donc à écarter pour désigner l'étude de l'emploi, à des fins grammaticales, des distinctions qui sont à la disposition des locuteurs.

Martinet makes it clear (in Hamm 1967:187) that he recognizes no distinct subject matter for morphonology or morphophonemics:

> I wonder whether we should not reserve the short term "morphology" for what has been presented as morphophonemics, or morphophonology, or morphonology. Why use the long word when we have a short word? From the modern structural stand-point we come to the conclusion that all problems relating to the value of the grammatical forms really belong to syntax in the larger sense of the word. This being so, the term morphology should be reserved for the study of the variations of all the "signifiants" of the language, and that would include whatever has been said about alternations (the so-called "morphophonological" alternations).

The idea that alternation is a proper part of morphology contrasts with the American descriptivist tendency to regard grammatically conditioned alternation as being predictable since it is redundant with respect to morpheme selection. European structuralism tends to give equal morphological status to all variation in form that correlates with difference in meaning. Hence, Jakobson, for example, handles nonautomatic alternation right along with the other aspects of morphology.[4]

A movement contrary to the general European trend is seen in the work of J. Kuryłowicz, who recognizes morphonology as an area of morphology (1968:79) and provisionally defines the morphoneme as (1967:161) "ein innerhalb eines morphologischen Ableitungsprozesses abtrennbarer Teilprozess, der vom phonologischen (diacritischen) Standpunkt relevant ist".[5] Kuryłowicz also speaks of "morphonemes (i.e. redundant morphs)" (1968:78) as "redundant elements" that are "semantically void" (81). One should note that, in accord with the inclusion of morphonology within morphology, morphonemes are not merely viewed as diacritic elements but also are given a status as morphological units.

But if alternation is taken as a proper part of morphology, then the basic principle of the morpheme itself must be reconsidered, and one must even ask whether a distinction can in principle be made between alternation and inflection; Kuryłowicz (1967:160) in effect raises the question:

> Wenn wir den idg. Ablaut e : Null, ei : i, eu : u usw. als morphonologisch bezeichnen, ist ein Gegensatz wie deutsch Tag : (Plur.) Tage auch als eine morphonologische und nicht als eine morphologische Tatsache aufzufassen?[6]

The question of the position of morphonology with respect to phonology and morphology is, of course, intimately tied to that of the relation between phonology and grammar. American descriptivists tended to
make a sharp division and to view phonology as being not only autonomous
but essentially independent from grammar;[7] this led to a compartmenta-
lized conception of language that easily allowed for morphophonemics as
a distinct area of investigation. European linguists, on the other hand,
were more inclined to stress the *connections* between phonology and grammar; L. Hjelmslev, who makes no specific comment on morphonology, represents this view (1939:54):

> Puisque dans la linguistique traditionelle la "phonologie" et
> la "morphologie" ont été toujours séparées par une cloison absolu-
> ment étanche, on a fermé les yeus sur les analogies entre les deux
> domaines, en s'empêchant ainsi d'en tirer profit des deux côtés. La
> linguistique traditionelle est prisonnière de l'illusion qui con-
> siste à croire que, si les faits de l'expression sont la plupart du
> temps restreints à agir à l'intérieur de leur propre plan, et sans
> avoir des répercussions sur le plan du contenu, les faits du con-
> tenu sont presque constamment en jeu sur les deux plans à la fois.
> C'est une erreur. Chaque plan a son organisation à lui il est vrai,
> mais chaque plan a des répercussions sur l'autre.

The interrelations of phonology and grammar are given special attention by Jakobson with respect to their bearing on morphophonemics:

> Any intended comprehensive study of a phonemic pattern inevi-
> tably runs into the problem of partial patterns mutually distingui-
> shing and specifying the diverse grammatical categories of the given
> language. The limit between phonemics proper and the so-called
> MOR(PHO)PHONEMICS is more than labile. We glide from one to the
> other imperceptibly. . . .

> The boundary between morphology proper and mor(pho)phonemics
> has proved to be vacillating. As soon as word grammar proceeds (in
> the terms of de Groot and Reichling) from the "structure of meaning"
> to the "form structure", we find ourselves in the domain of morpho-
> phonemics, because a purely formal analysis of paradigms means noth-
> ing other than the disclosure of the phonetic similarity and dis-
> tinctiveness of different paradigms, their members and components.
> Whatever we analyze, the sound or the meaning, if our analysis is
> linguistic, we necessarily discover with Bonfante and Pisani that
> the phonemic and grammatical structures present simply two aspects
> of one and the same indissoluble totality and are necessarily and
> intimately co-ordinated. And let us add with J. Lotz that the two
> structures present many striking similarities. [1971c:109-110]

While language is a single, "indissoluble totality", we nevertheless "discern two levels: the grammatical pattern of meaningful elements
and the underlying phonemic pattern of mere discriminatory marks" (113);
"neither does the autonomy of these two linguistic aspects mean indepen-
dence, nor does their co-ordinate interdependence mean a lack of autonomy" (111).[8]

Except in "Russian Conjugation" (1948), Jakobson does not work within the framework of morphonology or morphophonemics in his descriptive
writing;[9] in this respect he is typical not only of the Prague Circle
but also of Russian linguists in general. In a similar way, the Moscow
School, founded by F. F. Fortunatov, had an understanding of phonology
as "morpheme-phonology" from the very start, and thus had no need for a
distinction between phonology and morphonology. Ďurovič (1967:565-66)
summarizes the Moscow School's position:

> Obwohl die Moskauer Phonologen zweifellos von der Prager Pho-
> nologie inspiriert wurden, besonders von ihrer funtionellen Auffas-
> sung der Sprache, betrachteten sie das Phonem als einen Beŝtandteil
> des Morphems und identifizierten es nur über das Morphem, ohne Rück-
> sicht auf die durch Neutralisation hervorgerufene Identität oder
> Nichtidentität der einzelnen Laute. Die Folgerung dieser Konzeption
> war, daß hier das Problem der 'kombinatorischen Morphemveränderung-
> en', niemals existiert hat.
>   Und da die morphematische Einstellung der Moskauer Phonologie
> die Folgerung einer engen Bindung zwischen der phonematischen und
> morphologischen Ebene ist, ist es begreiflich, daß man hier die
> freien Alternationen immer als einen Bestandteil der Morphologie
> betrachtete.

Ďurovič also indicates (565) that R. I. Avanesov (1955, 1956ab) was
the first linguist in this school to apply the term 'morphophonemic' to
the type of transcription that had traditionally been called 'phonemic'.
Since this change there has been much discussion of morphonology in Soviet linguistics.[10] Most scholars have adopted morphonology while rejec-
ting the morpheme as a unit; A. A. Reformatskij (1955:99) states his
objection to the latter:

> In the search for a linear taxonomy, N. S. Trubetzkoy invented
> a nonexistent unit that is unnecessary for the structure of lan-
> guage—one without a correspondence in the objective reality of

language. There is a correspondence of alternation of variants of
morphemes (*ruk-* || *ruč-*; *beg-* || *bež-*; *son-* || *sn-*, etc.), but [k] ||
[č], [g] || [ž], and especially [o] || zero do not form any real units
of the structure of the language.

Thus, the concept of the 'morpho(pho)neme' is an unnecessary
concept that either imitates other concepts (Ułaszyn, Trager) or
else corresponds to a mythical object (Trubetzkoy, Swadesh).

The question of morphonology is much more complicated and serious.

Ju. S. Stepanov devotes an entire chapter (1966:110-17) to morphonology but works without the morphoneme as a unit (112):

> But the morphoneme as a special unit of language is a rather
> artificial construct. There is not evidence at all that morphonemes
> function as integral units; this is not justified by simplicity of
> description—the introduction of this notion even complicates the
> description. The majority of Soviet linguists do not accept the con-
> cept of the morphoneme.

O. Akhmanova, without reference to the same definition by Hockett,[11]
defines morphonology in terms of information theory as a code (1971:75):

> When the categories of information theory are invoked it seems
> possible to regard the morphonological system of a language as a
> code, which transduces, at the transmitting end, the flow of mor-
> phemes into a flow of phonological units. The same code would then
> be also responsible for the reverse process—the transduction of the
> flow of phonemes into morphemes at the receiving end.

But she remains skeptical of the need for morphonology as a distinct
area of linguistics and appears to adopt the position typical of other
European scholars (1971:79-80):

> Generally or theoretically speaking there is no reason whatso-
> ever why [alternations] should be made into the subject of a special
> linguistic discipline and not left to remain part of morphology, as
> they have always been in the case of morphology proper, i.e. the
> fact that so many linguists manage very nicely without so many more
> subdivisions of linguistics proves that there are no reasons, no in-
> trinsic reasons for setting them up.

:: :: ::

The European linguistic schools mentioned thus far in this chapter have for the most part taken explicit positions on morphonology and have used relatively familiar terminology in discussing the problem. British linguistics, therefore, presents special difficulties, since it offers little in the way of a specific evaluation of European morphonology or American morphophonemics and it uses a rather unique terminology that is likely to confuse linguists from a different background.

Within his theory of "prosodic analysis"[12] J. R. Firth (1948:150-52) draws a fundamental distinction between "prosodies" and "phonematic units". Robins (1957b:6) reports that "the latter are not phonemes or phonemic units, and the analysis is carried out in terms other than phonemic." Many examples of prosodic analysis are directed at phenomena termed "morphophonemic" by other scholars, and it is of considerable interest to note, for example, that K. H. Albrow (1962) treats the stem-final consonant alternations of Russian verbs in such a way that the alternating consonants are regarded as being phonematically identical but prosodically different. It is incorrect to identify prosodies as morphophonemic devices, however, since the postulation of the former generally does not rest on grammatical criteria. Thus, the vowels of the English pairs *goose : geese, mouse : mice*, and *hold : held* are phonematically the same and prosodically different, while those of *sing : sang* (and probably of *man : men*) are phonematically different since the phonematic assignment of English vowels is seen as depending only on their height. The extent to which grammatical factors are paramount as criteria for setting up prosodies remains an issue among Firthian linguists.[13]

Firth speaks of the distinctive sounds commutable in a given position as "substitution counters" (1935:10), but these seem to be the same as "alternants" when he says, "If we take an ordered series of English words or forms such as *bi:d, bid, bed*, . . ., we have sixteen vowel alternants in what may be considered the same context" (1936:40). Firth uses the term 'alternance' like 'alternation' and talks of the "morphological function" of alternance in English irregular verbs (1935:11). Such morphological function, as opposed to the minor (i.e. diacritic)

function of distinguishing shapes from each other, is the major function
of alternance (1936:541):

> In other words, the value of any letter [presumably, of the
> phonological calculus] is determined by its place in the context
> and by its place in the alternance functioning in that type of con-
> text. This I have called its *minor* function, but grammatical and
> semantic function must also be considered. These I have termed ma-
> jor functions.

Firth takes particular exception to American morphophonemics (1957b:
22):

> Some linguists seem to regard phonemics as a kind of pure math-
> ematics handling ultimate linguistic units, and morphophonemics as
> a kind of applied mathematics to prove morphemes. Such analysis does
> not go beyond the basic principle of linear and successive segmen-
> tation . . ..

His objection is directed not just at the notion of morphophonemics
but at the entire effort to make an exhaustive breakdown of utterances
into discrete morphological units;[14] Firth claims that "morphology as a
distinct branch of descriptive linguistics has perhaps been overrated,
owing to its very different place and value in historical linguistics"
(1957b:31). Such a position naturally was in harmony with an interest in
the "word-and-paradigm" (WP) model, which was touched on by Hockett
(1954:§1.1) in his comparison of "item-and-arrangement" (IA) with "item-
and-process" (IP):

> Quite apart from minor variants of IP or IA, or models that might
> be invented tomorrow, there is one model which is older and more
> respectable than either. This is the *word and paradigm* (WP) model,
> the traditional framework for the discussion of Latin, Greek, San-
> skrit, and a good many more familiar languages . . .. WP deserves
> the same consideration here given to IP and IA.

WP is examined in detail by R. H. Robins, who claims that "the long
maintained employment of WP type grammatical statement in Europe . . .
must argue for a certain conformity of WP with some of the commonsense
intuitive ideas of grammar and grammatical structure of which speakers
are themselves aware" (1959:118). Martinet also acknowledges the importance of WP description (1965:29):

> Les paradigmes de déclinaison et de conjugaison des grammaires tra-
> ditionnelles semblent être la façon la plus économique de rendre
> compte de la morphologie des langues classiques.

Of course, the sort of WP model in modern linguistics does not ig-
nore analysis below the level of the word, but since the morpheme is sub-
ordinate to the word in emphasis, the question of morphophonemics is put
in a different perspective; thus, Robins observes that "WP avoids some
of the difficulties in morphophonology (morphophonemics), in the relating of grammatical structuring to phonological structuring, which beset
IA (and to a lesser extent IP)" (1959:132). Such considerations play a
role in the attention that has again been given to WP and morphophonemics
in British linguistics by P. H. Matthews and in American linguistics by
Hockett.[15]

CHAPTER V

AMERICAN DESCRIPTIVISM AFTER BLOOMFIELD

Much continuity can be seen in the development of American descriptive linguistics from Bloomfield to the present day, but for the sake of
a practical grouping of material it is useful to distinguish a period of
American descriptivism after Bloomfield. No strong claim lies behind the
use of the term 'descriptivism' rather than 'structuralism', but the former term seems to fit the spirit of the period well.[1] Of course, many of
the linguists grouped here have continued to develop and modify their
views after the appearance of generative-transformational theory; their
later work is mentioned here or in Chapter VI, "Linguistics since Generative Grammar", depending on the issue in question. On the other hand,
some contemporaries of Bloomfield also belong to the mainstream of post-
Bloomfieldian linguistics and were not discussed in Chapter III, "American Linguistics through Bloomfield"; we shall turn to these linguists
next.

:: :: ::

Contemporary criticism of Bloomfield's theoretical framework exposed
certain contradictions involving phonemics and morphology. When linguists
set about to eliminate these inconsistencies and to perfect the Bloomfieldian system, issues were raised which led to a number of opposing alternative positions on each of two basic questions. Thus, on the one hand,
the effort to distinguish synchronic phonemics from morphophonemics led
to the issues of grammatical prerequisites and autonomous phonology.[2] On

the other hand, the contradictions in Bloomfield's views that morphemes were composed of phonemes and that morphemes could have variant forms raised the problem of morpheme alternants, morphophonemes as linguistic units, and item-and-process versus item-and-arrangement models. Taken together, the rejection of autonomous phonology and the adoption of the item-and-process framework supplied the principal ingredients for what developed into generative phonology.

The Rise of Autonomous Phonemics

The first aspect of Bloomfield's system to come under critical scrutiny was his phonemics. M. Joos (1967:96) provides us with a view in retrospect:

> When we look back at Bloomfield's work, we are disturbed at this and that, but more than anything else Bloomfield's confusion between phonemes and morphophonemes disturbs us. Bloomfield kept himself out of trouble here, usually, by describing just one language at a time, or one area within each at a time, adjusting for the effects of the confusion. But it made his procedure an unsafe model for neophytes and made the corpus of his work an inadequate source to distill procedural theory out of.

This question was discussed within a year after the publication of *Language* (1933) by a number of linguists. The article focused most directly on Bloomfield was "The Phonemes of Russian" by G. L. Trager, which takes response to Bloomfield's transcription of Russian as its starting point (1934:334):

> In Language 10.43ff. (1934), R. G. Kent, in his review of L. Bloomfield's Language . . . mentions Bloomfield's transcription of the Russian word for *city*, gorod. Bloomfield writes ['gorot], while Kent would prefer ['gorət]. The justification given to Kent by Bloomfield for his transcription is: 'Weakening of unstressed syllables in Russian is sufficiently indicated when the place of accent is given, i.e. ['gorot] but plural [goro'da] tells as much as ['gorət, gəra'da]: in fact, it tells more, since each of these transcriptions indicates both the accented and the unstressed forms of each vowel-phoneme, whereas ['gorət], for instance, fails to tell whether the second syllable has [o] or [a] or [i].'
> The words after 'whereas' have brought to my attention the question of a satisfactory representation of the unstressed Russian vowels from the point of view of a true phonemic transcription.

Although Trager does not define 'true phonemic', he decides (336)
that such a transcription is provided by neither Kent nor Bloomfield,
and he then provides an alternative analysis that deals with neutralization of the unstressed vowels in such a way that each "actual sound" is
transcribed in a single way (339-40):

> By this analysis, the actual present phonemic structure of Rus-
> sian vowels is clearly presented; the confusion between certain his-
> torically (and morphologically) distinct phonemes in atonic and pre-
> tonic position is shown; and we avoid both the use of more than one
> symbol for the same actual sound (except where differing structure
> permits the distinction into two phonemes) . . ., and the use of
> non-phonemic symbols which distorts the structural picture.

This suggests the principle behind Bloch's paper against overlapping (see below), but there is a catch in the sort of "differing structure" that would be viewed as permitting "the distinction into two phonemes". An inconsistency becomes apparent when Trager turns from the unstressed vowels to the problem of final devoicing of consonants and Bloomfield's transcription of ['gorot] with final [t] (340-41):

> Bloomfield writes the symbol for the voiceless sound, because
> voiced and voiceless sounds are separate phonemes in Russian. But
> we have seen that the same sound may belong to different phonemes
> if the conditions covering its use can be so described as to make
> clear the distinction. Now it is true that a comparison of the nom.
> sg. rod *kind* with rot *mouth* (both [rot]); of pop *priest* with rab;
> of mox *moss* with bog; of groʃ *farthing* with noʒ ; etc., shows no
> difference in the structure of the words; in each case the final
> sound appears under the same external conditions, and is voiceless.
> But let us take the genitives: roda [r'oda], rta; popa [pap'a],
> raba [rab'a]; moxa [m'oxa], boga [b'oɣa]; groʃa [graʃ'a], noʒa
> [naʒ'a]; we have a structural difference in the paradigm as a whole,
> and since the paradigm exists in the mind of the speaker as a psy-
> chological reality, there exists a psychological difference in the
> sounds found in the nominatives as well as in other forms. In such
> words as those cited, the phonetically voiceless finals resolve them-
> selves into two 'ideal' sounds, depending on other related forms of
> the words (cf. Sapir [1925], especially 45, note 2), and we have the
> phenomenon of a set of sounds, [p, t, x] etc., of some words, which
> is psychologically distinct from the exactly equal [p, t, x] etc.,
> of other words. The only proper phonemic transcription . . . seems
> to be one with the voiced symbols, the rule being that the sounds
> become voiceless in absolutely final position.

The difficulty is that the phonetic structure of the nominative singular forms of words showing the interchange is identical with that of
words that do not show it. So the notion of "structure" is interpreted
as including relations within grammatical paradigms. The psychological
background is clearly that of Sapir.

Another problem arises, however, when Trager considers stems derived
from those for which he has set up final voiced phonemes (on the basis of
an alternation) but which do not themselves involve any alternation. He
hesitantly proposes a criterion for setting up his "phonemic" forms that
is not unlike P. Kiparsky's later "alternation condition"[3] (341-42):

> I propose a double solution, fully conscious of the apparent
> inconsistency involved. For [some words] let us use the voiced sym-
> bols, since there exists at least one inflectional form of the word
> itself which retains the voiced sound. . . . For derivatives, how-
> ever, in which the original sound does not reappear in any inflec-
> tional form of the derivative, I propose the use of the symbols for
> the unvoiced sounds.
> The rule for voiced stops and spirants is this, then: the ety-
> mological voiced sounds . . . retain their psychological identity
> and distinction from the corresponding voiceless sounds in final
> position or before a voiceless sound in all words in which at least
> one inflectional form retains the original sound, even though they
> are, objectively, completely voiceless in the positions indicated;
> but in derivatives under the same conditions, where the original
> voiced sound does not reappear in any inflected form, we have com-
> plete psychological identification of the original voiced sound
> with the new, voiceless sound, and their merging into the voiceless
> phoneme, despite the presence of the voiced sound in the original
> of the derivative, or in some other derivative.

Trager felt that the principles presented in his paper enabled him
to make a sharp distinction between "phonemics" and "morphophonemics"
(344):

> If, then, we say that interchanges between sounds are phonemic
> when the conditions governing them are purely phonetic or phonetic
> and structural, and are morphonemic only when they are conditioned
> by purely morphological facts without any change in the descrip-
> tively valid phonetic conditions, we have justified our discussion
> of certain Russian consonant changes as a purely phonemic problem
> of the same general kind as that involved in certain vowel inter-
> changes.

But this claim can be misleading because it takes 'morphophonemics'
in a narrow sense that excludes phonetic conditioning. Trager freely uses
this term and 'morphoneme' (335) and expected his reading audience to be
familiar with them. He provides no definitions of the terms, but it is
clear that he was introduced to them by writings of the Prague Linguistics Circle.[4]

Writing in the same volume of *Language*, M. Swadesh indicates in
"The Phonemic Principle" (1934) that his view of "morpho-phonology" derives from Trubetzkoy and Ułaszyn (117); he presents the first general
discussion on the subject by an American (128-29):

> Morpho-phonology includes, in addition to the study of the pho-
> nemic structure of morphemes, the study of interchange between pho-
> nemes as a morphological process. If a given morphologic interchange
> is sufficiently regular and characteristic, the interchanging pho-
> nemes may be regarded as a morphologically unitary set. Examples are
> Indo-European e/o/ē/ō/zero, English f/v (in, e.g. *leaf*, *leaves*).
> Whether it is a convenient fiction or a true reflection of linguis-
> tic psychology, morphological processes are usually described as
> having a definite order. *Leaves* is taken to be a secondary formation
> from *leaf*, and in consequence v is the mutation of f and not f that
> of v. But f does not always change to v in the morphological process
> of plural formation; thus, we have *cuff*, *cuffs*. The f of *cuff* is
> therefore morphologically different from the f of *leaf*, though pho-
> nemically it is the same entity. Morphologically, we have two f's
> so that $f_1:v::f_2:f$. Morphologically distinct phonemes are called
> morpho-phonemes.
>   A morpho-phoneme is one of a class of like phonemes considered
> as components of actual morphemes which behave alike morphological-
> ly, i.e., have a like place in the same mutation series. The morpho-
> phoneme is never to be confused with the phoneme as such even in
> the event that all instances of a given phoneme are members of the
> same morpho-phonemic class. One may devise a morphologic writing
> for use in morphological discussion or in a dictionary, but such a
> writing is not to be employed in ordinary linguistics records.

As in the early Praguean view, the morphophoneme is regarded as an
entity (here, as a set) rather than as a descriptive device. Swadesh,
like Trager, tries to make a separation between phonology and morphonology, but difficulties become apparent in his discussion of transcription.
At first Swadesh is willing to assign scientific status only to phonemic
transcription (124-25):

> A phonemic orthography provides the most adequate, economical and effective method of writing a language. Morphological and grammatical study of a language and the recording of its conclusions looks to orthography as an instrument of fundamental importance. A phonemic alphabet is the only kind that is truly adequate, for it alone represents all the pertinent facts and only the pertinent facts.

But it seems he is reacting primarily against overly narrow transcription. As he elaborates the principles to be followed in transcribing he shows his readiness to allow morphophonemicized ("normalized") phonemics.[5] First he presents a general discussion of alternation that is of interest on its own account (118-19):

> The word sometimes has regular variant forms; in this event, two forms may differ as to one or more phonemes though they are in a sense the same word. Since variants sometimes confuse the phonemic problem, it may be well to point out some of the types of variants:
>
> I Free variants (either variant is equally correct in any position)
>   A Particular (applying to a single word or a limited number of isolate words), e.g. . . . Eng. *economics* . . ..
>   B General (applying to all words of a given class) . . ...
> II Conditional variants (determined by position in the sentence)
>   A Particular, e.g. Eng. *a, an*
>   B General
>   (a) Phonetically conditioned . . .
>   (b) Structurally conditioned, e.g. Tunica disyllabic words of the form CVʔV have that form only when spoken in isolation; in context they become CV . . ..
> Conditional variants may be regular . . . or may be optional, as the Eng. sandhi type of *as you* [az yu, až(y)u], both of which are sometimes interchangeably employed by the same speakers.

Then Swadesh faces the question of how variant forms of words are to be transcribed (126):

> When two or more forms of a word are both correct, two courses are possible, namely to record the form employed at each given time, or to always write one of the variants. The latter treatment is called normalization. In the case of particular word-variants, normalization would have to be entirely arbitrary and is therefore to be avoided. In the case of optional general variants, it is usually possible to normalized without obscuring the fact of variation. This is possible when one can so define one's symbols that the affected phonemes in such a variation are readable in two ways. For example, one may write äz yu for English 'as you', and indicate as part of the definition of the symbol z that before y it may have the value ž, the y being sometimes then lost. . . . Similarly, in the case of

phonemic interchange, one may write the distinctive form and mention the interchange in the definition of the phonemic symbol.

So it appears that Swadesh's notion of phonemics, like that of Trager, is mixed with what later came to be identified as morphophonemics. Much of the difficulty in being consistent about phonemics—and this applies to the entire period from the 1930's up to the present—has lain in making a clear distinction between phonemic analysis and the various sorts of transcription that could be employed for various purposes. Y. R. Chao touches on this in a footnote to the reprinting in Joos (1967:38) of his article, "The Non-Uniqueness of Phonemic Solutions of Phonetic Systems" (1934):

> Since this was written at a time when the differences between transcription and phonemicization and between phonemes and morphophonemes were not as clear as they are today [i.e. ca. 1957], the article would have to be reworded in many places if these differences were to be taken into account.

The practical aspects of problems in transcription contribute to the highly pragmatic character of Chao's avowed aim (38):

> The main purpose of the present paper is to show that given the sounds of a language, there are usually more than one possible way of reducing them to a system of phonemes, and that these different systems or solutions are not simply correct or incorrect, but may be regarded only as being good or bad for various purposes.

Chao shows a wordly understanding for the conflicts that arise in attempts to hold fast to a set of rigid criteria for phonemic analysis (49):

> The list of phonemes shall not only be exhaustive for the language, but, other things being equal, we should try to make the membership of the classes mutually exclusive. Other things, hoever, are never equal, and we have in fact already allowed the possibility of over-lapping of membership between phonemes. . . .

Chao then proceeds to a general discussion of phonemic overlapping; he confronts the problem of morpheme variants and indicates two possible solutions.[6] Characteristically, however, he points to alternatives and refrains from taking a rigid position[7] (49-50):

The use of symbols has two aspects, the aspect of reading, or
the determination of the object from the given symbol, and the aspect of writing, or the determination of the symbol from the object.
The reading aspect of phonemic symbols is always determinate with
respect to the language in question. Given a phonemic symbol, the
range of sounds is determined, and the choice within the range is
usually further determined by phonetic conditions. It would also be
a desireable thing to make this reversible, so as to include the
aspect of writing; that is, given any sound in the language, its
phonemic symbols is also determined. If phonemes do not overlap,
this is obvious. If they overlap, and the common members occur under
different phonetic conditions, the reversibility still obtains. . . .
But if the identity of a common member between phonemes is unconditional . . ., then it would be impossible to go from the sound to
the symbol even for the native speaker. Strictly, a non-reversible
symbolization of sounds based on etymological or other considerations becomes an orthography and ceases to be a transcription . . ..
In other words, homonyms should not have different transcriptions.
There is, however, a class of intermediate cases, where the common
member between two phonemes occurs sometimes under exactly the same
phonetic conditions, but at other times becomes differentiated in
some way under other sets of identical conditions. . . . The reversibility is therefore only partial. Usage is by no means uniform in
such cases. Sometimes, symbolic reversibility is secured at the expense of word identity, the same word . . . appearing in two forms
. . . considered as different sets of phonemes. At other times identity of word form is secured at the expense of reversibility.

As Chao indicated, phonemic practice among American linguists in the
1930's varied considerably, but few people made an effort to avoid the
sort of irreversibility he had described. C. F. Voegelin is typical of
the trend when he simultaneously assigns a single allophone to two different phonemes under identical conditions (1935:55):

From hearing a single word which contains ŏ it is impossible to
tell to which phoneme the vowel belongs; but when hearing the word
under different accentual conditions, the phonemic affiliation becomes clear.

A number of fundamental questions had been raised or suggested: What
are the criteria for phonemic analysis? What is its methodology? What is
the best way to transcribe? But few answers had been offered. The situation changed in the early 1940's when articles appeared by younger linguists who sought to establish definite guidelines for phonemic theory
and practice. In "Phonemic Overlapping" B. Bloch concentrates on the problem raised by Chao but seems to be unaware of the latter's discussion

(1941:278):

> I do not know of any published work that has even posed the
> question—important as it is both in practice and in theory—whether
> phonemes may intersect: whether a given sound, that is, may belong
> to two or more different phonemes in the same dialect.

Bloch makes a distinction between partial and complete overlapping
(279):

> The intersection or overlapping of phonemes will be called
> partial if a given sound x occurring under one set of phonetic con-
> ditions is assigned to phoneme A, while the same x under a different
> set of conditions is assigned to phoneme B; it will be called com-
> plete if successive occurrences of x under the same conditions are
> assigned sometimes to A, sometimes to B.

Unlike Chao, however, he takes a definite position:

> Partial intersection . . . can never lead to uncertainty in
> practice and may therefore be admitted in theory without violating
> sound phonemic method. The same cannot be said, however, of complete
> intersection. Examples are rare, and are always the result of an er-
> ror in the analysis. [281]

> In short, a system in which successive occurrences of a given
> sound x under the same conditions must be assigned to different pho-
> nemes necessarily breaks down, because there can be nothing in the
> facts of pronunciation—the only data relevant to phonemic analysis
> —to tell us which kind of x we are dealing with in any particular
> utterance. [283]

Bloch's paper, clear and concise, possesses an almost magic ability
to charm and convince the reader. One wonders how any position other than
his could be possible. But the paper also has a faint air of sophistry
to it, and the apparent *necessity* of Bloch's view provides a key to understanding this. The whole question of whether complete overlapping is
permissible in phonemics turns less on a problem of what phonemics *is*
than on the methodological question of what the term 'phonemics' is to
be applied to; put roughly, not a fact but a definition is in question.[8]
Bloch does not mention that a different definition of 'phonemics' could
be compatible with complete overlapping. But if there is a fallacy behind Bloch's argument, it is far from obvious. Most linguists of the time
were more involved with the grosser mistake of confusing analysis with
transcription. Joos (1967:96) characterizes the article and its effect:

It was the present article by Bloch that made clear, as it never had been before, that phonemics must be kept unmixed from all
that lies on the opposite side of it from phonetics: kept uninflu-
enced by the identities of the items of higher rank (morphemes and
so on) that their identities entail, such as their meaning and their
grammar.

A few years later Z. S. Harris (1944a:§4.1) introduced the term 'biuniqueness' to cover Bloch's principle of excluding complete intersec-
tion:

Finally, if we are ready to admit partial overlapping among
phonemes, we may agree to have different components in different environments represent the same phonetic value. So long as we do not
have a component in one environment represent two phonetic values
which are not freely interchangeable, or two components or component-
combinations in the same environment represent the same phonetic value, we are preserving the bi-unique one-to-one correspondence of phonemic writing. (The term bi-unique implies that the one-to-one correspondence is valid whether we start from the sounds or from the
symbols: for each sound one symbol, for each symbol one sound.)

From this aspect of phonemic methodology, C. F. Hockett came to the
generalization that grammar was to be excluded from phonemics. The position is presented in a series of terse statements in his article "A System of Descriptive Phonology" (1942a):

No grammatical fact of any kind is used in making phonological
analysis. [§10.1]

There must be no circularity; phonological analysis is assumed
for grammatical analysis, and so must not assume any part of the
latter. The line of demarcation between the two must be sharp.
[§10.2]

Hockett's position provoked a reply from K. L. Pike, "Grammatical
Prerequisites to Phonemic Analysis", which argues that "it is impossible
for such claims to be realized completely, and that even were it possible
it would at times prove undesirable" (1947a:155). Pike continues (155):

To eliminate the facts of grammatical relationship and structure from the analysis and presentation of phonological structure
is frequently undesirable because many of the phonological facts
are inextricably interwoven with grammatical facts and structural
relationships; avoiding the portrayal of this relationship means
omitting, completely or at least temporarily, an important part of
the total structure of the language.

Pike takes particular exception to what he sees as inconsistency between Hockett's theory and practice (159):

> There must be something wrong with present-day phonemic theory if workers agree on the practical value and validity of a procedure (and of evidence) in the field which they then rule out in theoretical discussion and in presentation.

Hockett defends his own use of grammar in phonemics as being non-circular, e.g. (1950:69-70):

> We have been led to this rephonemicization through grammatical considerations; but once discovered the new analysis is established purely on phonological grounds . . ... Grammatical considerations can serve as *clues* for phonological analysis without implying that the latter is *logically* built on the former; there are still no grammatical 'prerequisites' for phonemic analysis.[9]

Pike in turn claims that there is no vicious circularity in his method of simultaneously analyzing phonemics and grammar (1952:120):

> Such a procedure need not be circular; rather it is a *spiral* procedure, building higher conclusions on earlier conclusions and data, moving where necessary from one type of data to another and back again.

The problem of grammatical prerequisites was closely linked with the question as to whether or not juncture[10] was an essentially grammatical feature. E. Haugen surveys the debate (1951:§3.7):

> [In phonemic analysis] we have no criterion for identifying phonemes until we have determined their environment, and no way of determining the environment until we have identified the phones. Since morpheme boundaries are part of the environment, there appears to be no good way of entirely isolating phonemic and morphemic analysis. Leopold [1948] has shown that in German one either has to analyze such words as *Frauchen* and *Kuhchen* into two morphemes first or else leave the palatal and velar spirants of *ich* and *ach* as separate phonemes. Pike's [1947] contention that morphological criteria must be admitted into phonemic analysis seems to be inescapable unless one can find external, objective criteria which will tie either the phonemes or the morphemes to some specific reality.

These issues go to the very heart of phonemic theory, and a full discussion exceeds the scope of a work primarily directed toward morphophonemics. But they are of fundamental significance for morphophonemics, and

the fact that linguists reached no consensus continues to have its effect.
The lack of agreement stemmed in part from the failure to agree on the
precise issues at stake, as Hockett (1955:3) observes:

> Certain investigators, among them Pike, believe that in order
> to understand a phonologic system it is necessary not only to know
> certain things about the accompanying grammatic system, but to make
> active use of the latter knowledge as criteria for phonologic dis-
> cussion. Others disagree. But the issue is not clear: in actual
> fact, we are probably in covert disagreement as to what our overt
> disagreements are about.

Hockett now feels[11] that a misunderstanding arose partly because he
and others failed to see the full significance behind the fact that Pike
had given his book *Phonemics* (1947b) the subtitle *A Technique for Reducing
Languages to Writing*. From the very outset Pike's aims were essentially
practical: he sought a method for arriving as quickly as possible at the
most efficient transcription for describing a language. 'Phonemic' was
the epithet he applied to such a transcription.

Hockett's rejection of grammar from phonemic analysis—whether or
not such a goal could be attained—had nothing to do with convenience of
procedure but followed *necessarily* from his understanding of phonemics.
His basic distinction between phonemics and morphophonemics is well illustrated in a passage by Joos (1967:92):

> The native listener may be said to perceive—to somehow exploit
> for message-understanding ends—items in what he hears. Insofar as
> this process does not depend on understanding, the items are phonem-
> ic; insofar as items cannot be perceived without understanding, mor-
> phophonemics at least (perhaps more) is involved. I borrow an ex-
> ample from C. F. Hockett: Once he heard someone say 'She has poise'
> and, momentarily insufficiently attentive, innocently said 'What's
> a poy?' The phonemic items had been apprehended perfectly, but,
> through a lapse in understanding, the morphophonemic items had not.

The criticism of Pike's understanding of 'phonemics', furthermore,
does not mean that Hockett denies morphophonemic transcription a use in
grammatical description (1947b:§5):

> A notation is phonemic if it indicates, in every position, only
> those phonemic contrasts which occur in that position, but indicates
> all of them. Once one has found the morphemically most desirable pho-
> nemic notation, one can often handle certain additional simple mor-

phemic problems by modifying it in such a way that, in addition to
indicating unambiguously all the phonemic contrasts occurring in a
position, it also indicates in certain positions contrasts which
are *not* there phonemic.

Bloch (1950:122-24) echoes these remarks and is more emphatic in
stressing the suitability of morphophonemic transcription for practical
purposes:

> Only one kind of written record, according to Bloomfield [1933:
> 85] is scientifically relevant: 'a record in terms of phonemes, ig-
> noring all features that are not distinctive in the language'—and
> ignoring also, if the record is to be strictly phonemic, all fea-
> tures that are distinctive but not immediately observable in the
> stream of speech, such as morpheme boundaries, word structure, and
> morphophonemic relations. Such a record is the only safe and ade-
> quate basis for further investigations of linguistic structure; the
> analyst who attempts to study the morphemes for the grammatical con-
> structions of a language in terms of a transcription that is either
> less or more than phonemic—a raw phonetic transcription on the one
> hand, or on the other a transcription that tacitly relies on non-
> phonetic evidence—will either be lost in a confusion of irrelevant
> details or overlook significant correlations between the phonemic
> structure and the structure of the other linguistic levels. . . .
>   However, it does not follow that a rigorously phonemic tran-
> scription must be retained throughout all the levels of a descrip-
> tive treatment. . . . Once the transcription has been used in the
> study of morphemes (in particular, of morphophonemic alternations),
> it may be   legitimately modified, elaborated, or normalized . . ..
> A normalized notation, still firmly based on the phonemic analysis
> but incorporating the most common or the most important morphopho-
> nemic relations—especially those that are automatic—and such gram-
> matical features as word boundaries and pitch morphemes, approaches
> the character of a practical orthography. It is usually far better
> adapted to the discussion of morphology and syntax than a wholly un-
> modified transcription.

The question of "grammatical prerequisites" gradually shifted to one
of "autonomous" versus "systematic" phonemics, but the basic issue and
its relevance for morphophonemics remained much the same. The criticism
of Bloomfield's phonemic practice had led—at least among linguists who
shared the views of Bloch and Hockett—to a more narrowly and sharply defined sense of 'phonemics'; "morphophonemics" was largely understood in
a negative and relative sense as a kind of pseudo-phonemics that went beyond the limits of "true" phonemics. But morphophonemics occupied a cen-

tral position in post-Bloomfieldian descriptivism and must also be seen
in relation to developments in the area of morphology.

Definitions of 'Morphophonemics'

We mentioned in Chapter III that an inconsistency was involved in
Bloomfield's claims that (1) all morphemes are forms, (2) all forms are
composed of phonemes, but (3) some morphemes "have" different "forms"
depending on their environments. The inconsistency rested on the nontechnical use of 'form' in (3).

Laying heavy emphasis on procedural steps, Z. S. Harris (1942) introduces a distinction between "morpheme alternants" and "morpheme units"
that resolves the problem:

> We divide each expression in the given language into the smal-
> lest sequences of phonemes which have what we consider the same mean-
> ing when they occur in other expressions, or which are left over when
> all other parts of the expression have been divided off. . . . The
> resultant minimum parts we call not morphemes, but *morpheme alter-
> nants*. [§2.1]
>
> From the list of morpheme alternants which results from the pre-
> ceding step, we take any two or more alternants which have what we
> consider the same meaning (but different phonemes) and no one of
> which ever occurs in the same environment as the others. The two or
> more alternants which meet these conditions are grouped together in-
> to a single *morpheme unit* . . .. [§2.2]

Harris realizes that more than one way of defining the morpheme is
possible. One alternative is to say that morpheme units *are not* composed
of phonemes but that they have different shapes—morpheme alternants—
which are. Another alternative is to say that morphemes *are* composed of
phonemes but are invariant in shape, so that the total stock of morphemes
in a language is multiplied (1946:§2.2):

> We may say that each morpheme can have only one phonemic form,
> so that for example the English plural endings /s/, /z/, /əz/ (as in
> *books, chairs, glasses*) constitute three morphemes, and *am, are* con-
> stitute two morphemes. Alternatively, we may include each of these
> sets in a single morpheme, if we say that different phoneme sequences
> constitute positional variants of one morpheme when they are comple-
> mentary to each other.

Most linguists, including Hockett, adopted the solution provided by morpheme alternants. He later introduced the term 'morph' on an analogy with 'allomorph' (1947b:§2):

> The utterances of a language are examined. Recurrent partials with constant meaning . . . are discovered; recurrent partials not composed of smaller ones . . . are *alternants* or *morphs* ["A convenient term, because it (1) eliminates the lengthy expressions 'morpheme alternant' and 'morpheme unit', and (2) suggests a valid analogy (allo)phone : phoneme = morph : morpheme."]

E. A. Nida (1948:§3.02, fn. 13) actually proposed the term 'allomorph'[12] and modified the sense of 'morph':

> Morphemic alternants can conveniently be called *allomorphs*. Accordingly, allomorphs are related to morphemes as allophones are related to phonemes. In the process of analyzing a language there might be occasion to use the term *morph* to designate a structural unit which has not yet been assigned to any morpheme; but in the description of a language (as distinct from the procedure of analyzing it) every structural element except features of arrangement is either a morpheme or part of a morpheme. Hence every element is also an allomorph or part of an allomorph.

The distinction of allomorphs from morphemes brought attention to a new area of linguistic study that Hockett variously defined in a succession of works:

> The branch of grammar which deals with the phonemic shape of morphemes, words, and constructions, without regard to their meaning, is *morphophonemics*. [1942a:§10.1]

> Some morphemes appear in more than one phonemic shape, depending on phonemic or morphemic environment; the statement of such alternations is called morphophonemics. [1947a:274]

> The differences in the phonemic shape of alternants of morphemes are organized and stated; this constitutes *morphophonemics*. Morphophonemic statements may involve morphophonemes—that is, the symbols used for phonemes, plus supplementary ones, with special definitions as to phonemic value under varying circumstances—or they may not; often lists are more convenient, and sometimes they are unavoidable. But regardless of the methods used in describing them such alternations are morphophonemic. [1947b:§2]

One should note that the last two definitions are narrower than the first, identifying morphophonemics with differences between the shapes of morphemes rather than with their shapes in general. Other linguists fol-

lowed in adopting the narrower sense; one definition[13] is given by Bloch:
"Morphophonemics is the study of the alternation between corresponding
phonemes in alternant shapes of the same morpheme" (1947:§7.1).

Another narrow definition is formulated by R. S. Wells (1949:99-100):

> When the utterances of a language have been analyzed into their
> smallest meaningful units, the morphemes, a number of these morphemes
> in most languages have more than one morpheme alternant. Insofar as
> these alternants are sequences of phonemes (in which case we call
> them morphs), the phonemic differences among all the different morphs
> belonging to one phoneme can be described, classified, and compared
> with the differences among morphs of other morphemes, considered mor-
> pheme by morpheme. The total class of these differences so described,
> classified, and compared is called the *morphophonemics* of the lan-
> guage in question, and any two morphs of the same morpheme are said
> to stand in a relation of (morphophonemic) *alternation* with each
> other.

Well's article is an attempt to codify the part of morphophonemic
theory dealing with automatic alternation, which he also defines (100-1):

> Given that a morpheme has, say, two alternants A and B, their
> alternation is automatic if the environments in which A occurs, and
> those in which B occurs, can each be characterized in purely pho-
> nemic terms.[14]

Wells shows great methodological care, and a number of his observa-
tions are useful, such as the designation of cases like Sanskrit *rabh* +
ta = *rabdha* as 'reciprocal conditioning' (109). Other terminology is introduced here, such as 'narrow' and 'wide static alternation' (105-8),
but none of it was generally adopted. The articles's style is rather for-
bidding, and in retrospect one wonders how many linguists made the effort
to give it a careful reading.

Bloomfield (1939:§2) had narrowed the definition of 'morphophonemics'
in another way by identifying it with internal sandhi. Nida (1946:200)
follows this convention and speaks analogically of external sandhi as
'syntactophonemics',[15] but Harris (1942:§4.2, fn. 17) had already argued
against separating internal and external sandhi when they can be treated
together.[16]

Later, however, the notion of 'morphophonemics' was again taken in
a broad sense by Hockett (1950:63):[17]

Morphophonemics, as the term is used here, subsumes every phase
of the phonemic shape of morphemes: the typical shape of alternants,
the types of alternation, and the various environmental factors
(phonological or grammatical) which elicit one alternant or another
of those morphemes which appear in more than one shape. This usage
is broader than some which have recently been described, for in-
stance by Bloch [1947] and by Wells [1949].

This definition implies that morphophonemics occupies a place in the
design of every language (63):

Every language has morphemes, and so every language has morphophonemics. In the conceivable limiting case, the morphophonemic section of a description would consist of a single statement: each morpheme appears, wherever found, in one and only one phonemic shape.
Probably no such language exists.

The broad sense is evident in a definition by Trager and Smith, who
use the term 'form' nontechnically and fail to distinguish morphophonemics from the lexicon: "The statement of all the forms of the morphemes
of a language is the morphophonemics" (1951:54). The intention is clarified in a later passage (60):

A full study [of English morphophonemics] would involve statements about the kinds of consonant and vowel sequences that occur,
the relation of certain stresses to specific segmental phoneme structure, and the relation of intonations to the stresses and junctures;
then would follow a morpheme list with all allomorphs, and an indef-
initely extendable list of morphemes not showing alternation.

The last sentence above implies that in the strict sense, automatic
alternations were not alternations at all for Trager and Smith.

Defining morphophonemics was intimately connected with understanding
the design of language for Hockett. The notions of 'mechanics' and 'tactics' play a central role here; 'mechanics' appears early (1940:55):

Mechanics. Today it has become the fashion to collect into one
place all the mechanical details of formative process—the specific
internal changes involved in each type of ablaut, the secondary modifications accompanying affixation, and so forth—and to devise a
set of symbols by which these changes may be abbreviated, and by
which any regularities that underly apparent irregularities may be
emphasized.

The term 'tactics' comes later in a statement on design (1947a:281):

> [The method proposed] has the merit that it permits a clear
> division between two echelons of description: morphophonemics, which
> accounts for all submorphemic changes in phonemic shape of morphemic
> units; and tactics, which states the arrangement of morpheme units
> in words (or in utterances) without concerning itself with submor-
> phemic variations.

Hockett (1948a:185) then speaks of a division of grammar into "mechanics" ("phonetics, phonemics, morphophonemics") and "tactics" ("morpheme classes and their positions of occurrence"). He does not adopt this
division but mentions it in comparison with his own view (1954:§2.11):

> Morphophonemic and tactical pattern taken together constitute
> *grammatical pattern*. This, paired with *phonological pattern*, com-
> pletes the synchronic pattern of a language. The cleavage between
> phonology and grammar is thought by some (including myself) to be
> more fundamental than that, within grammar, between morphophonemics
> and tactics, even though, for some purposes, other stratifications
> are possible. For example, it is sometimes convenient to class mor-
> phophonemic and phonological facts together, say as 'mechanics', in
> collective contrast to tactics (Hockett 1948[a]:185). Or, if the
> distinction between automatic and non-automatic morphophonemics is
> made . . ., it also makes a good deal of sense to class automatic
> morphophonemic facts with phonology, non-automatic with tactics . . ..

A still more generalized view of morphophonemics was gradually developed by Hockett. He offers one definition in glossematic terms (1951:
341 fn.):

> If I follow Hjelmslev's discussion at all, his 'expression'
> level is my 'phonological' . . . and his 'content' level, so far as
> it is worked out in terms of form and not of substance, is my 'tac-
> tical'. My 'morphophonemics' is then the set of rules which relate
> expression and content.

Later he defines it as a sort of code:[18]

> Under this view, then, morphophonemics becomes not the way in
> which different morphs, in different environments "belong to" one
> and the same morpheme, in the sense that elements belong to a class,
> but rather the complicated code governing the phonologic representa-
> tion of morphemes and morpheme sequences.[19] [1955:15]

> The ways in which the morphemes of a given language are vari-
> ously represented by phonemic shapes can be regarded as a kind of
> code. This code is the *morphophonemic system* of the language. [1958:
> 135]

The morphophonemic system is in turn presented as one of "the three central subsystems" of a language (1958:137):

    (1) The *grammatical* system: a stock of morphemes, and the arrangements in which they occur;

    (2) The *phonological* system: a stock of phonemes, and the arrangements in which they occur;

    (3) The *morphophonemic* system: the code which ties together the grammatical and the phonological systems.

From this understanding it follows that "the morphophonemics of a language is never trivial; any systematic description of any language must cover it" (1958:135). But Hockett issues a warning that the morphophonemic system is not independent of the others[20] (1958:142):

> An act of speech does not have a "morphophonemic" structure. Morphophonemics resides entirely in habits, and is manifested not by another variety of structure in historical events, but by interrelationships of the two varieties of structure already itemized.

While it has been claimed above that Hockett developed a "broad" definition of 'morphophonemics', it is extremely important to note that he chooses to exclude all grammatically functional (i.e. significant) formal differences from his understanding thereof. He likewise takes 'alternation' in a narrow sense that excludes the relation between English *sing*, *sang*, and *sung*, which is the phenomenon for which the term was introduced[21] and for which it still is used by many linguists, e.g. R. A. Hall, Jr. (1964:138):

> In phonemically different shapes of allomorphs, the phonemes which differ are said to *alternate* with each other or to be *in alternation* (as when /I/ alternates with /æ/ and with /ə/ in /sɪŋ sæŋ səŋ/ *sing, sang, sung*. . . .
> An alternation of phonemes within a given morpheme bridges the gap between the morphological and the phonemic levels, and hence is called *morphophonemics*. . . .
> In the broadest sense of the term, morphophonemics includes all alternations of phonemes within morphemes, whether these alternations are predictable (automatic) or not, and whether they are meaningful or not.

Definitions of 'Morphophoneme'

No definition of 'morphophonemics' in writings by Harris from this period has come to my attention.[22] The omission is noteworthy and symptomatic of the differences in approach between Hockett and Harris. Hockett, in turn, does not define 'morphophoneme' directly, while Harris gives a series of definitions, the first of which appears in his sketch of Hebrew (1941a:153-54):

> In some cases a large number of morphemes have analogous variants in the same environment. The relation of the one variant to the other in each of these morpheme-units can then be stated in a single formula. Such a formula tells us that the morphemes concerned will have a particular phoneme (or phoneme combination) when they are in one environment, but another phoneme (or phoneme combination) when they are in a different one. This replacement of one phoneme by another may occur in all morphemes in the indicated situation . . . or it may occur in a particular group of morphemes . . ..
>
> The phoneme, or phoneme combination, or absence of phoneme, which is replaced by the other phonemes in the variants of a morpheme-unit may be called a morphophoneme. The following morphophonemic formulas [23] . . . show in what conditions each phonemic replacement occurs. In the remaining environments, which the formula does not describe, it is the unreplaced phonemic value of the morphophoneme that occurs.

The morphophoneme is presented here as a "real" entity—specifically, as a phoneme in a certain morphological function; the influence of Uła-szyn[24] seems apparent. One should also note that the definition depends on the notion of "replacement".

Methods in Structural Linguistics (1951a) contains a number of definitions, which appear, however, to be contradictory. Harris seems to depict the morphophoneme as a "real" unit (219):

> Now that some morphemes have phonemically different members, it is of interest to know whether we can recapture the state of having all members of a morpheme identical. By definition, this could not be done in terms of the phonemic composition of the members, so that the problem becomes one of setting up new elements, replacing the phonemes, which will satisfy this requirement. These new elements would represent the features common to the various members of the morpheme for which they are defined.

But the passage hangs on the sense of 'represent', and it turns out that this has nothing to do with Hockett's technical usage but instead involves the idea of transcription (225):

> We take a morpheme written as a combination of symbols which do not change no matter what the environment. In each environment, each symbol represents the phonemic composition which the part of the morpheme occupied by the symbol has in that environment. Such a symbol is called a morphophoneme.

Harris adds a definition of 'base form' (226):

> The new one-spelling morphophonemic writing of the previously plurimembered unit is sometimes called the base form or theoretical form, from which the phonemically written members are derived.

So far, everything is fine; but in a survey of results at the end of the book, Harris abandons the definition of the morphophoneme as a symbol and replaces it with one based on classes (362-63):

> Morphophonemes are classes of corresponding segments in stretches of speech which are equivalent in their morphemic composition. . . .
> The interchange of phonemes or components in corresponding sections of the variant members of each morpheme can then constitute a class called a morphophoneme. . . .
> We may therefore say that each morpheme is composed directly of a sequence of morphophonemes, each of which in turn is a class consisting of one or more complementary phonemes or components. Each morpheme has only one morphophonemic constituency but the distinctions between sounds are in general only in one-many correspondence with the distinctions between morphophonemes: two distinct morphophonemic sequences may represent identical segment (or phoneme) sequences; such different morphophonemic sequences are phonemically equivalent.

Special Symbols

Whether or not the morphophoneme was to be understood as a class of phonemes, its definition was related to the problem of specifying the role of "special symbols" in a description. Harris (1942:§5.4) summarizes Bloomfield's technique in "Menomini Morphophonemics"[25] and then gives a step-by-step account of the considerations involved in deciding whether it is practical to employ morphophonemic symbols (1951a):

> In order to have a single composition, i.e. a single spelling,
> for all occurrences of a single morpheme, it is often necessary to
> resort to elements which represent the various phonemic compositions
> of the morpheme in its various environments. In some cases these el-
> ements may be merely redefinitions of phonemic symbols (redefined
> as a one-many correspondence); in other cases new symbols have to
> be defined. [232]

> When it is impossible to differentiate phonemically between the
> morphemes in which an alternation occurs and those in which it does
> not, or between the environments of the one member of the alterna-
> tion as against the environments of the other . . ., and when the
> environments in question are not some small class of morphemes which
> could be listed, then it is most convenient to define new morphopho-
> nemic symbols to indicate the occurrence of the alternation. [230]

> In some cases there is in general no advantage to identifying
> morphemes as composed of morphophonemes instead of phonemes.
> One such case is that of morphemes all of whose members are
> phonemically identical. . . .
> Another such case is that of morphemes which have more than
> one phonemically distinct member, but the alternation among which
> members is identical with no other alternation. [238]

> When an alternation appears in very few morphemes, it depends
> upon convenience and upon our purposes whether we indicate it by a
> morphophoneme or by a list of members alternating in a morpheme.
> [239]

Hockett tries to use the notion of special symbols to help clarify
the nature of automatic alternation (1947b:§6, fn. 19):

> We are forced to use capitals or some other device for evanes-
> cent vowels, because other vowels, phonemically the same, are not
> evanescent. This fact marks these alternations as *non-automatic*.
> Where no extra symbols are needed—where the symbols already used
> phonemically are merely extended to positions in which they do not
> phonemically occur—the alternations are *automatic*.[26]

This echoes the early distinction made by Swadesh and Voegelin (1939)
between "patent" alternations, statable in terms of phonemes alone, and
"non-patent" alternations, whose description is most easily accomplished
with special symbols representing grammatical or lexical as well as phonetic information.

But the employment of special morphophonemic symbols led to contro-
versy. Bloomfield used different symbols to distinguish a segment which
alternated from one which did not. Such a phonetically unmotivated dif-

ference of notation, however, could also be used to distinguish one segment as a conditioning factor from another, phonetically identical segment that did not condition an alternation. This means that covert morphological features might be expressed by special symbols in a morphemic
transcription, while overt features corresponding to the actual differences of the pronounced forms would not be expressed in the morphemic
transcription but would be derived later through the application of morphophonemic rules. A similar situation in Bloch (1947:407) is criticized
by Nida (1948:§2.2):

> The past tense form /sæŋ/ is treated as an alternant of /siŋ/.
> The meaning-difference is considered as expressed by a zero suffix.
> By this procedure an overt distinction—the replacement of /i/ by
> /æ/—is treated as meaningless, while the covert distinction be-
> comes the meaning-carrier. I do not deny the significance of zero
> in such a form, nor the importance of the pattern which leads one
> to recognize a zero; but it appears to me as strikingly contradic-
> tory to treat overt distinctions as meaningless and covert distinc-
> tions as meaningful.

Nida opts for a treatment in terms of replacive morphs and then proposes principles to ensure an adequate morphemic analysis with regard
to overt differences between forms.[27]

Reduction of Alternations

Besides the use of morphophonemic symbols or lists, other new devices were applied in morphemic analysis. Since Chao, linguists like
Hockett had been aware of the possibility of alternate phonemic analyses
and notations:

> It has not been proved that the phonological system presented
> in this paper is the correct one, or even that there is just one
> correct phonology. [1942a:§10.2]
>
> The phonemic structure of the language is that which remains
> invariant under all possible transformations from one sufficient
> phonemicization to another. [1949: fn. 6]

Hockett points out that the alternatives in choosing a phonemiciza-
tion could have a bearing on the identification of allomorphs and the de-

scription of alternations[28] since "we may discover that a phonemic notation other than the one we have used—for there are always several mutu-
ally convertible possibilities—would simplify the task" (1947b:§4). One
such alternative involves a rephonemicization in terms of components,[29]
as described by Harris (1944a):

> From the point of view of relations between allophones, this
> operation means that we extend complementary distribution to apply
> not only to single allophones but also to sequences of allophones.
> From the point of view of the physical nature of allophones, it
> means that we no longer require an allophone to be an observable
> complete sound; we extend the term to include observable components
> of a sound. [§5.3]

> Such components are especially worth extracting if many mor-
> phophonemic statements are thereby eliminated . . ... This will in
> general happen only in cases of automatic morphophonemic alterna-
> tion. [§6.2]

Harris then summarizes the technique (1944a:§7):

> Defectively distributed phonemes complementary to sequences of
> phonemes are broken up into allophones of those sequences. Limita-
> tions of phonemic distribution, including neutralization, cluster
> limits, and certain automatic morphophonemic changes, are resolved
> by components having a length of more than one phoneme.

An example is found in Harris 1945b:§1.5.

Morphophonemics and Internal Reconstruction

All the various techniques involving componential analysis and special symbols resulted in notational systems that bore little resemblance
to phonetic transcription.[30] In particular, the use of morphophonemic
symbols often resulted in a kind of transcription that seemed more like
an historical reconstruction than a synchronic representation of the language under investigation.[31] This similarity was not merely an accident
of notation but reflected a relationship that had been touched on early
by Swadesh and Voegelin (1939:2):

> Alternations are the result of phonetic history, affected also
> by foreign borrowings and analogical changes. The most efficient
> formulation of the synchronic facts is ordinarily not the same as

a reconstruction of the actual historical developments, but the process of constructing morpho-phonemic formulae has some resemblance to that of historico-phonological reconstruction.

Linguists realized that the parallelisms between morphophonemics and internal reconstruction had significance for the methodology of the latter, as indicated by Hockett (1958:463):

> Many morphophonemic irregularities found in a language at a given stage reflect an earlier regularity disrupted by phonemic restructuring. Therefore, a careful examination of morphophonemic irregularities in a language, and of the distributional aspect of its phonological system, should yield reasonable deductions about its earlier history.

An actual codification of methodology for internal reconstruction is presented by H. M Hoenigswald (1944, 1946, 1960); one passage may serve as an example of how alternations constitute the basis for arriving at such reconstructions (1946:§4):

> Compulsory automatic alternation between restricted /x/ and free /y/ in a paradigm indicates a previous conditioned sound change from /x/ to /y/ in the position from which it is now excluded. The reconstruction is often supported by the existence of parallel non-alternating paradigms showing only /y/. Mod. Ger. /d/ is restricted in comparison with /t/, in that it does not occur in syllable-final position . . .. Moreover, /d/ and /t/ are in compulsory alternation in such paradigms as /búnde/ Bunde . . . : /búnt/ Bund . . .. From this state of affairs the merger of the syllable-final allophone of /d/ with an allophone of /t/ . . . could be inferred even if it were not known from historical records.[32]

Hoenigswald (1946:§7) summarizes the basic assumptions underlying internal reconstruction. One should note the identification of alternations (insofar as they are not disturbed by analogy) with the results of sound change; the passage also suggests the view that languages have essentially agglutinative morphology that is more or less obscured by analogical changes:

> This analysis of sound changes and their effect on the pattern of a language rests on such general linguistic assumptions as the regularity of phonetic change and the phonemic principle, and is therefore believed to be applicable to any kind of language structure. By distinguishing reversible processes (i.e. those which leave unambiguous traces behind) from ambiguous ones, it furnishes the

rules of *internal reconstruction*, a method which supplements or (in
the absence of comparative data) substitutes for comparative reconstruction. It is worth noting that unambiguous traces necessarily
involve the distribution of sounds in morphological paradigms: com-
pulsory alternants permit the reconstruction of conditional merger
between phonemes. . . . Rules such as these (which have been tested
though not formulated by generations of linguists) imply that the
analogical processes and syntactical constructions whereby meaningful forms (morphemes, words, clauses) are put together, are essentially regular, i.e. statable in terms of order and selection, while
alternation is brought about by sound change (and then again frequently abolished by new analogical handling of forms) . . ..

This close relationship of alternations with sound shifts enables
Hockett (1948c:§4) to speak of Bloomfield's morphophonemicized transcription of Algonquian languages as involving a "preliminary internal reconstruction". Just as cognate relationship had served as Baudouin's basis
for grouping alternants together,[33] alternation conversely was now used
in a passage by J. W. Marchand (1956:246) for identifying cognate morphs:

> The basic problem in IR [internal reconstruction] is to find
> a means of discovering cognate morphs, and a means of testing the
> findings. In IR, the problem of the discovery of cognate morphs is
> solved for us by a synchronic description of the morphemics. It may
> be said that all the allomorphs of a morpheme are cognate with each
> other, unless suppletion has occurred. . . .
> If one or more phonemes regularly alternate, under any condi-
> tions whatsoever, with one or more other phonemes in the same mor-
> pheme, these phonemes must have derived from the same phoneme or
> group of phonemes, or else suppletion has taken place . . .; if two
> allomorphs are cognate, they must stem from one and the same mor-
> pheme of a previous stage of the language, existing in one phonemic
> shape. In such a case we say that phonemic split has taken place.

Of course, none of the above linguists made an unconditional *identification* of morphophonemics with internal reconstruction; F. G. Lounsbury notes their differences and also rejects agglutinative structure as
a universal (1953:§1.1.3):

> Morphophonemic constructs cannot be said to represent a previ-
> ous stage of the language. Although strictly agglutinating languages
> doubtless have existed . . . there are no grounds for supposing that
> every language has descended from such a forebear simply because it
> is possible to construct an agglutinating morphophonemic analog to
> it. But that the morphophonemic transformation formulas set up often
> correspond to actual historical sound changes of some variety cannot

be doubted. Such an assumption is the basis for historical reconstruction from internal evidence. The reason for the invalidity in
considering morphophonemic constructs as historical forms lies in
the fact that the morphophonemic rules correspond to historical
changes of different types, which occurred during widely different
periods of the history of the language. Some correspond to sound
changes that have affected the phonetic pattern of the language as
a whole and are of the type known as phonetic laws. Others correspond to analogical changes that never of themselves altered the
phonetic pattern at large, but which were confined to specific morpheme combinations. . . .

But morphophonemics and internal reconstruction are similar enough
in methodology that Lounsbury chooses to disregard their differences and
apply the term 'internal reconstruction' to both (1953:§1.1):

Two general approaches to these problems [segmentation and
grouping] may be recognized in the history of modern linguistics.
One of these, the older of the two, has sometimes been known as the
morphophonemic approach, because of the so-called 'morphophonemes'
. . . which are sometimes employed instead of ordinary phonemes in
the identification of morphemes. This usage is confusing, however,
for the term 'morphophonemic' has other more common meanings in
contemporary descriptive linguistics . . .. We shall call it, instead, the method of internal reconstruction, for whether the orientation be historical or avowedly synchronic, it is usually based
on an operation which is similar to that of reconstruction from internal evidence.

Item-and-Arrangement and Item-and-Process

In making an identification of internal reconstruction with morphophonemics, Lounsbury had taken a narrow sense of the latter and regarded
it as one of two basic approaches to the description of alternations; in
this view "morphophonemics" involved the use of theoretical base forms
and processes in terms of them. The other approach rejected these devices
and instead worked in terms of alternants and their distribution. These
two fundamental methods involved not only the description of alternations
but reflected basic alternative methods in the description of language as
a whole.[34]

One can speak loosely of such 'approaches' or 'methods', but the
standard expression is 'model', as explained by Hockett (1954:§1.1):

By a 'model of grammatical description' is meant a frame of
reference within which an analyst approaches the grammatical phase
of a language and states the results of his investigations. In one
sense, there are as many models as there are different descriptions
('grammars' in the sense of monographs). But in another, and very
important, sense, most grammatical descriptions seem to cluster about
a relatively small number of relatively distinct models; it is with
these archetypal frames of reference that we are concerned here.

For the two models most prominent in contemporary linguistics Hockett (1954:§1.1) introduced the names 'item-and-process' (abbreviated 'IP')
and 'item-and-arrangement' (abbreviated 'IA'). IA and IP were not limit-
ed to the description of alternations, but the dichotomy was so clear in
this area that it assumed a central place in discussion over the two models.

An example of IP that shows its implications for morphology in general as well as for alternation is to be seen in an early paper by Hockett (1942b:2):

> Form v3s [3rd singular] is derived from vr [root] by adding the
> suffix /-z/, with some phonetic modifications. The regular modifi-
> cations are that if vr ends in /s z š ž č ǰ/ the vowel /ə/ (/e/ or
> /i/ in some dialects) is inserted before the suffix; if vr ends in
> a voiceless consonant other than /s š č/ the /z/ is changed to /s/:
> /kət : kəts, sîj : sîjz, kác : kácəz/.

This passage closely follows the principles of Bloomfield's *Language*. One immediately notices words like 'derived', 'adding', 'modifications', 'inserted', and 'changed' that mark the model.

There was no problem of choosing between IA and IP for Bloomfield
and Sapir because all American linguistics of the 1930's and earlier followed IP. The distinction did not appear in the linguistic literature until the mid-1940's in Harris's review of Newman's description of Yokuts.
Harris first notes that the work is in fact based on a process model; he
also distinguishes the latter from an historical framework (1944b:198):

> The difference between two partially similar forms is frequent-
> ly described here as a process which yields one form out of the
> other. Thus when bases or themes have several vocalic forms, the
> various forms are said to be the result of vowel-change processes
> operating upon the base or theme . . . .. The difference between a
> base and a base-plus-suffix is described as the result of the pro-
> cess of suffixation . . . .. This is a traditional manner of speaking,

especially in American Indian grammar (e.g. in the Handbook edited
by Boas). It has, of course, nothing to do with historical change
or process through time: it is merely process through the configuration, moving from one to another or larger part of the pattern.
Although . . . such terms are less used today, they fit in very well
with the method used by Newman, because this system is in general
modelled on moving systems.

Harris then indicates that a process model can be replaced by one
based in terms of elements and their distribution (203-4):

> [A] term that is disappearing today, no doubt under the influence
> of Bloomfield's Language, is "process." There is involved here a
> method, not merely a term. Newman uses "process" to indicate a re-
> lation between two forms one of which may be viewed as consisting
> of the other plus some change or addition. Thus, the addition of
> suffixes to a base is a process, as is the assimilation of a pre-
> glottal-stop vowel to the quality of the vowel after the glottal
> stop . . ., and the changing of vowels when suffixes are added. All
> such cases can be viewed differently, without bringing in the time
> or motion analogy implicit in "process." . . . We now have not a
> process from base to word via suffixation, but an inventory of the
> elements (morphemes) present in two utterances. . . .

The alternative solutions Harris describes avoid reference to "process or change" and instead "give us a number of elements, so defined
that when these elements occur next to each other their phonemic forms
are what we actually hear" (204). While Harris abandons the process model,[35] he takes all the alternative distributional solutions to be equivalent (1945b:§2):

> The phonemically different forms of one morpheme may be each
> considered a complementary positional variant of the morpheme. Al-
> ternatively and equivalently, base forms can be constructed, whose
> constituents are not phonemes but morphophonemes, and from which, in
> each environment, the appropriate variant of the morpheme can be de-
> rived by substituting for the morphophonemes the appropriate pho-
> nemes (following stated rules).

Elsewhere he expressly states that he does not intend the newer model as a replacement for the older (1947 II: fn. 12):

> It should be clear that description in terms of morpheme alter-
> nants in no way replaces description in terms of morphophonemes. Al-
> though some cases can be equally conveniently treated in either man-
> ner, morpheme alternants are used primarily in cases in which mor-
> phophonemic treatment is not convenient.

The IP methods of Sapir and Bloomfield involving morphophonemes and rules, however, were themselves still quite new to linguists. *Linguistic Structures of Native America* (1946), the famous collection of grammatical sketches by H. Hoijer et al.,[36] is full of process-type morphophonemics. M. B. Emeneau borrows the technique of Bloomfield 1939 in his grammar of Kota (1944:17):

> Phonological operations take place on two descriptive levels. morphological elements (morphemes) are set up in theoretical base forms, the minimum distinctive segmental units of which are the morphophonemes. When morphemes are combined to form words, replacements of morphophonemes may take place in the descriptive passage from the morphophonemic to the phonemic level. Statements of such replacements are morphophonemic operative rules . . ..

Reviewing Emeneau's work gives Harris the opportunity again to present the newer model, while also recognizing the merits[37] of IP descriptions (1945a:285-86):

> The model used by Emeneau in this analysis is probably the clearest way of treating morphophonemic phenomena, and most convenient for many languages. It is worth noting, however, that it is possible to present the same facts in quite a different manner. Instead of using the model of base forms composed of morphophonemes, it is possible to speak directly in terms of the observable morphemes and phonemes. We then say that each morpheme is composed of phonemes, but that in some cases we find two or more morphemes which are complementary to each other and function distributionally as one morpheme. We therefore treat these two or more as positional variants of one functional morpheme and state in what environment each variant occurs. If the difference between the variants affects only one or two phonemes, we may accept one variant as being primary, and say that when the given morpheme (in its primary variant) occurs in a particular environment, these phonemes are replaced by others. This parallels the non-automatic morphophonemic or external sandhi rules. If the difference appears in all morphemes which have a particular phoneme or phoneme sequence, we say just that, and so parallel the automatic rules. . . . The whole morphophonemics and sandhi thus becomes a series of statements about variants of morphemes.

Both models struck Harris as having certain merits; his view that practical considerations could determine the choice between the two rested on the premise that IP[38] as well as IA reduced to a distributional basis (1954:149):

The combinatorial or item style, which has a more algebraic
form, is more parsimonious and representative for much linguistic
data. The process style, which is more similar to historical statements, is useful in certain situations, especially in compact morphophonemics ["best expressed in the work of Sapir and Newman"].
Both styles are based solely on the relative occurrence of parts,
and are therefore distributional.

Such a reduction of process in terms of distribution is shown in the
format of "automatic morphophonemic lists" presented in *Methods*.[39] Each
row of the list is a statement descriptively equivalent to one of the
structure "element *1* is replaced by element *2* in the environment *3*", but
Harris avoids all reference to "replacement" or other processes (1951:
376):

1. Every morpheme which contains the following phoneme or phonemic sequence when it is not in the environment of col. 3	2. has (instead) the following phoneme or phonemic sequence	3. when it occurs in the following environments.

Objection to the IP model rested largely on the opinion that it was
itself historical or at least derived from an historical bias.[40] Wells
(1949:112) states the view:

The preference for the dynamic conception is due to the predom-
inantly historical interest of most linguists, especially during the
19th and early 20th centuries. When morpheme alternants were described, linguists were motivated by their historical interest to
choose as basic that one which they believed to be primitive; or if
they believed neither to be primitive, they . . . constructed a non-
existent form . . .. The metaphor of change in synchronic linguistics in general is favored by the same ultimately historical, diachronic interest.

While not agreeing with Well's interpretation, Harris sees the similarity of synchronic to diachronic processes as an advantage of IP (1951b:
290):

The process model has the advantage of being more dramatic and
often of reflecting the actual historical changes. . . . It has the
greater advantage of opening the way to a more subtle descriptive
analysis—something always dear to Sapir's heart—by giving a special secondary status to some parts of the descriptive structure.
. . . On the other hand, the process model has the disadvantage of

bringing into descriptive analysis a new dimension—which does not
fit well into the algebraic character of the present bald statements
of distribution. There is need for further elaboration of descriptive techniques, in order to make room for such refinements among
our direct distributional statements.

But Harris observes—in contrast to his other claims of equivalence
of the two models—that IP introduces a "new dimension" that does not fit
the framework of IA. The same objection had already been made more strongly by Hockett in his review of Nida's *Morphology*[41] (1947a:282):

> If 'morphological process' and 'phonological process' were sec-
> ondary terms, introduced as convenient shorthand to avoid constant
> repetition of long statements containing the primary term 'morpheme'
> there could be no objection. But in Nida's presentation 'morpholog-
> ical process' is just as fundamental as 'morpheme'. We don't need
> both.

Here the attention is directed not so much toward process techniques
used in describing the morphophonemic alternation of morphemes but rather
toward processes that are essentially morphological in character and that
displace the morpheme as a theoretical unit. The effort to develop a
method of pure IA description stemmed not from a conviction that IP had
no advantages but from an effort to arrive at "primitive" (or "primary")
terms of morphological analysis. Hockett's lack of bias is evident[42] in
a passage where he considers factors that had led to the emphasis on IA
(1954:§1.7):

> It seems to me that the current general preference for IA rath-
> er than IP—and such a prejudice is certainly observable—stems at
> least in part not from any great excess of merit of IA over IP, but
> rather from the following: (1) We like, nowadays, to be as formal as
> possible. (2) IA has been formalized, and IP has not. It is unfair
> to compare a formalized IA with an informal IP and conclude that the
> former is better just because it is formalized. If it could be shown
> that IA is capable of formalization but that IP is not, that would
> be another matter. But . . . I hope to demonstrate that no such
> claim can be made.

Alternative models were sought by Hockett since they aided in high-
lighting the parts of a language that gave the linguist true options in
a description as opposed to the parts that forced a solution (1947b:§25,
fn. 38):

> Our aim is to achieve the most accurate and clearest picture
> possible of the workings of a language . . .; in some cases this is
> attained not by giving a single treatment, but precisely by indi-
> cating the alternatives. For in some cases a range of choice is de-
> termined not by our approach, but by the nature of the language; and
> when this is so, the existence of a range of choice in a particular
> portion of the language is one of the facts about the language that
> ought to be portrayed in our description. . . .

Hockett's concern with IA versus IP is partially directed toward
their bearing on morphophonemics. Within this area he notes a group of
problems that are troublesome for IA (1954:§4.1):

> Most morphophonemic problems find simple answers in IA, for
> there is available a wide variety of morphophonemic techniques all
> well within the bounds of the IA model. However, there is a refrac-
> tory residue, troublesome not because no solution can be found, but
> either because a multiplicity of solutions present themselves, no
> one seeming much better than another, or because the intuitively
> best solution is clearly in violation of the fundamental orienta-
> tion of IA. This residue includes such cases as *took*, *put* (past
> tense), *children*, French *bon* and *bonne* . . ..

The IA model favors a solution in terms of discontinuous and infix
morphs for the past tense of *take*, but Hockett finds an analysis involving replacement—or subtraction to derive *bon* from *bonne*—to be intui-
tively more satisfying. Since such solutions belong to the domain of IP
(in that "replacive" and "subtractive" morphs do not consist of phonemic
material as required by IA), he concludes that, for at least some facets
of description involving morphophonemics, IP is superior to IA (1954:
§7.3):

> IP obviates the major tactical and the major morphophonemic
> difficulty of IA. We are not confronted with superfluous machinery
> in the case of *baked* or *took*: the process involved is singulary, so
> that the only factors are the respective underlying forms and the
> process. The morphophonemic difficulty which IA gets into with *took*
> is obviated, since the whole frame of reference is one in which the
> difference between *took* and *take* is just as acceptable as that be-
> tween *baked* and *bake*.

The above passage and others in the same article present views that
are now generally associated with transformational grammar (§3.0):

> A grammatical description built according to the plan outlined [above] sets forth principles by which one can generate any number of utterances in the language; in this sense, it is operationally comparable to the structure of that portion of a human being which enables him to produce utterances in a language; i.e. to speak.[43]

Of course, it was not Hockett's intent to favor the IP model as a whole any more than IA; he concludes (1954:§7.5) that both models as presented have serious deficiencies. But the basic ingredients of generative grammar's approach to phonology and morphophonemics were available by the early 1950's; the most essential of these ingredients were a formalized IP model and the view of phonology that allowed "grammatical prerequisites" and the complete overlapping of phonemes. Linguistics was already moving toward formalization with mathematical models, and Hockett (1948a: 185) imagines the result of the development:

> As descriptive linguistics approaches maturity, structural descriptions will in time assume such a succinct and exact form that no one would think of *reading* one any more than a mathematician would read a table of logarithms; in that gloomy millenium, the comparison of structural types will be simple and obvious.

:: :: ::

Other issues, not directly bearing on morphophonemics, were also in ferment. Linguists were increasingly concerned with the form of a description and the criteria for its evaluation. The issue of "God's truth" versus "hocus-pocus"[44] made linguists unsure of the object of their studies and the nature of their activity. Some linguists were prepared to argue from the effectiveness of a morphophonemic description to its "truth" as a "theory"; Swadesh and Voegelin (1939:10) provide an early example:

> If it has been possible, by the recognition of a non-patent phonology involving two morpho-phonemic types of consonants and two of vowels and a set of mechanical rules, to reduce the apparent irregularity of Tübatulabal phonology to system, this very fact guarantees the truth of our theory. Truly irregular alternations could note be reduced to order.
>
> The value of a phonological theory is in direct proportion to the extent of its application, in inverse proportion to its complexity.

The following chapter will attempt to show how some of these issues are reflected in subsequent work on morphophonemics. But this carries us into the near past and the present, so that little claim can be made to providing comprehensiveness or historical objectivity. What follows is given largely for the sake of perspective to what has preceded. Morphophonemics had fully emerged as an area of linguistic investigation in the course of the periods surveyed thus far; subsequent discussion either produced only relatively minor developments or else—in the case of generative phonology—a rejection of the entire dichotomy between phonology and morphophonemics.

CHAPTER VI

AMERICAN LINGUISTICS SINCE GENERATIVE GRAMMAR

Chomsky's *Morphophonemics of Modern Hebrew*

Long before the publication of Hockett's "Two Models of Grammatical Description"[1] the challenge to produce a formalized process model was taken up by Noam Chomsky in his master's thesis, which was written under the direction of Harris. This work, *Morphophonemics of Modern Hebrew* (1951), will be discussed in some detail here since it is generally unknown but is quite revealing with respect to the historical development of generative grammar.

From his training under Harris, Chomsky naturally was familiar with the principles of descriptive linguistics as it was practiced in America. But other factors in his background have to this day been ignored or underestimated by many linguists. In the first sentence of the thesis Chomsky states that the study "has its roots in two fields, symbolic logic and descriptive linguistics"; specifically, Chomsky means "the constructional part of philosophy which uses logic as its essential tool", and he cites R. Carnap 1928 as an example. While "logical syntax" was not intended as a technique for the grammatical description of natural languages, Carnap (1935:41-42) presents principles remarkably similar to those adopted by Chomsky in his view of generative grammar:[2]

> When we say that the objects of logical syntax are languages, the word "language" is to be understood as the *system of the rules* of speaking, as distinguished from the acts of speaking. Such a language-system consists of two kinds of rules, which we will call formation rules and transformations. The formation rules of a certain

language-system *S* determine how *sentences* of the system *S* can be
constructed out of the different kinds of symbols. . . .
    The totality of the formation rules of a language-system *S* is
the same as the definition of the term "sentence of *S*." . . . Now
for a natural language, such as English, the formation rules can
scarcely be given completely; they are too complicated. . . .

Apart from the basic conception and formal techniques of logical
syntax, another influence on Chomsky is to be seen in the work of the
philosopher N. Goodman. Although Chomsky does not attempt in his thesis
to define rigorously the criteria that govern the formulation of grammatical statements, he asserts that "the statement of the grammar, the
presentation of the completed distributional analysis, must meet . . .
criteria which involve, essentially, considerations of elegance and considerations of adequacy as determined by the particular purposes of the
grammar" (4). Chomsky goes on to argue that "the considerations of elegance cannot be regarded as trivial or merely 'esthetic'" (4-5) and then
quotes from a passage by Goodman (1943:107):

> The motives for seeking economy in the basis of a system are
> much the same as the motives for constructing the system itself. A
> given idea *A* need be left as primitive in a system only so long as
> we have discovered no relationship intimate enough to permit defin-
> ing *A* in terms of them; hence the more the set of primitives can be
> reduced without becoming inadequate, the more comprehensively will
> the system exhibit the network of interrelationships that comprise
> its subject-matter. Of course we are often concerned less with an
> explicit effort to reduce our basis than with particular problems
> as to how to define certain ideas from others. But such special
> problems of derivation, such problems of rendering certain ideas
> eliminable in favor of others, are merely instances of the general
> problem of economy. Thus it is quite wrong to think of the search
> for economy as a sort of game, inspired by an abnormal love of su-
> perficial neatness. Some economies may be relatively unimportant,
> but the inevitable result of regarding all economy as trivial would
> be a willingness to accept all ideas as primitive at the outset,
> making a system both unnecessary and impossible.

Keeping in mind the influence of these two philosophers (the only
authors cited by Chomsky in his thesis), we can proceed to outline the
contents of the work. Chomsky distinguishes between "synthetic" (small
units to big, bottom to top) and "analytic" processes (big to small, top
to bottom) (2) and indicates that his description will involve the latter

type (3). In a statement of purpose he outlines the structure of his grammar and reveals its fundamentally generative character (6):

> The purpose of the grammar outlined in this paper is to specify,
> in terms of phonemes (ultimately, in terms of phonetic units), all
> the sentences of Modern Hebrew. The grammar is composed of syntax,
> morphophonemics, and phonemics. The introductory syntactic statement
> breaks down the sentence into its parts. The morphophonemic state-
> ment specifies these parts in terms of phonemes. The phonological
> statement effects the transfer from symbolism to observable fact.
> Thus the grammar is a set of analytical statements each of which an-
> alyzes more closely the units presented to it by the preceding state-
> ment. Running through the list of statements in one way (i.e., with
> one set of choices) gives one sentence. Running through them in all
> possible ways gives all possible sentences.

Thus, contrary to its title, the work sketches a complete description. Chomsky indicates that "certain parts . . . are only given in outline, or merely mentioned" (this applies especially to the phonology, in
the then-current sense, which is omitted entirely); Chomsky continues
(3-4): "But all of the essentials have, I think, been included, and a
complete description of Modern Hebrew, from this point on, would be
largely a matter of additional detail."

Pages 9-18 are devoted entirely to syntax. The model employed is
formalized and clearly generative, but the distinction made in *Syntactic
Structures* between phrase-structure rules and transformations is not in
evidence. As the presentation is highly compact, this section contains a
good deal of material, which should be of interest to anyone wishing to
study the historical development of Chomsky's views on syntax.

The remainder of the thesis (19-69) deals with morphophonemics.
Chomsky takes morphophonemes to be the units which compose morphemes (19).
The general form of the morphophonemic section and, in particular, the
general form of rules is discussed (22):

> The following set of some forty statements is, essentially, the
> definition . . . of the totality of morphemes in terms of their con-
> stituent phonemes. The statements are ordered, and, in general, the
> order is immutable . . .. Even within statements, substatements are
> ordered. . . . The statements have the form of rules of transforma-
> tion. Given a sequence of a certain shape, they direct you to alter
> the shape in a specified way. If the directions are followed, any
> sequence of morphemes . . . will be transformed step by step into

a sequence of phonemes.
    The typical statement is written in the form:

    K → L in env.: R—S, where....

    The interpretation of this is as follows: if the sequence RKS
occurs, and if the conditions specified by .... obtain, then 'RKS'
is to be rewritten 'RLS'.

Other notational conventions are then introduced before the bare
statement of the actual morphophonemic rules (27-46).

The following section is of particular interest and centers on the
question of rule odering.[3] Chomsky states the issue:

    The fundamental question about this preceding grammatical state-
    ment, aside from the question of its adequacy in describing the
    facts, is: in accordance with what general considerations was it
    constructed the way it was, and, in particular, to what extent is
    an order imposed upon the statements by these considerations? It
    will now be shown that the statements are, to a large degree, ordered
    by the criteria of 'elegance'.

He then proceeds to identify further the criteria of elegance[4] (49-
50):

    The general considerations which have been regarded as relevant cri-
    teria are as follows:
        1. Simplicity of statement.
        2. Maximization of the number of derivations in which a state-
           ment will occur relevantly.
        3. Minimization of irrelevant applications.
        4. Maximization of similarity among statements, and amalgama-
           tion of statements involving the same elements.

Whereas earlier descriptions in terms of ordered morphophonemic
rules, e.g. Bloomfield 1939, had been content merely to specify *sufficient* conditions of ordering (i.e. by arranging n rules in a linear order from 1 to n),[5] Chomsky's thesis attempts to specify *necessary* ordering and regards the set of morphophonemic rules as being only partially
ordered. The "necessary ordering" is presented in a chart on page 48,
from which one can see, e.g. that the order of application of rules *3* and
4, and of *5* and *6*, respectively, is not specified, while *3* and *4* must be
applied before *5* and *6*, and the order of *3, 4, 5, 6* is immaterial with
respect to the application of rule *9*.

Having presented the morphophonemic rules in a sufficient ordering in the linear listing of pages 27-46, Chomsky goes on to establish the necessary ordering by justifying each of the ordering constraints presented in the chart. He does this as follows: letting 'R' stand for 'rule', if the chart indicates that R_i precedes R_j, Chomsky assumes the reverse and then either (1) derives an incorrect form, or (2) shows that the ordering of R_j before R_i violates the elegance criteria presented above;[6] for each case this then establishes the necessary ordering of R_i before R_j. Chomsky (1964:71) indicates that the "depth" of ordering thus demonstrated reaches the range of 20 to 30.[7]

The Emergence of Systematic Phonology

For all its innovation in techniques, Chomsky's thesis does not really depart from basic conceptions of morphophonemics then prevalent. While taking the morpheme to be composed of morphophonemes (rather than phonemes), it does not question the American descriptivist phoneme as a unit. The phoneme appears not to be challenged even in the later review of Hockett's *Manual of Phonology* by Chomsky (1957b:225-26):

> One important and useful feature of Hockett's theory of speech communication is his view of various levels of linguistic description as distinct systems of representation related by general correspondences. Thus morphemes are not literally composed of phonemes; rather, morphemic and phonemic representation are two ways of coding utterances, related by morphophonemic rules. There is no need to identify a certain sequence of phonemes as the phonemic content of each morpheme. We are free to relate these levels by whatever rules can be most simply formulated, without imposing this rather arbitrary notational requirement.

Thus, the descriptivist dichotomy of phonemics and morphophonemics remains intact in some of Chomsky's early work. But the principle of biuniqueness and the rejection of "grammatical prerequisites", which formed the foundation of this dichotomy, were already questioned by Chomsky, Halle, and Lukoff (1956):

we believe that morphological and syntactic considerations may be
relevant to the preparation and evaluation of a phonemic transcription, and we do not require that the phonemic transcription provide
a unique representation for each utterance. [67]

It is . . . questionable whether the biuniqueness condition should
be taken as a requirement for phonemic transcription at all. [79]

Syntactic Structures (1957a) still takes a rather neutral position;
in elaborating his conception of morphophonemics Chomsky clearly allows
for a distinction between morphophonemes and phonemes:

Suppose that by a . . . grammar we can generate all of the
grammatical sequences of morphemes of a language. In order to complete the grammar we must state the phonemic structure of these morphemes, so that the grammar will produce the grammatical phoneme sequences of the language. But this statement (which we would call the
morphophonemics of the language) can also be given by a set of rules
of the form "rewrite X as Y", e.g. for English . . . *take + past*
→ /tuk/ . . ., etc. [32]

The elements that figure in the rules . . . can be classified
into a finite set of levels (e.g., phonemes and morphemes; or, perhaps, phonemes, morphophonemes, and morphemes) each of which is ele-
mentary in the sense that a single string of elements of this level
is associated with each sentence as its representation on this level
. . .. [33]

In the type of transformational grammar proposed here, the morphophonemic rules apply to the output of the transformational rules
and thereby convert strings of words into strings of phonemes. [46]

Phonemic identity is essentially complete rhyme . . .. [99]

But Chomsky adopts the principle of "grammatical prerequisites" and
goes on to argue that "opposition to mixing levels, as well as the idea
that each level is literally constructed out of lower level elements, has
its origin in the attempt to develop a discovery procedure for grammars"
(59); his understanding of phonology is therefore closer to Pike's than
that of the Bloch-Trager-Hockett group.

Chomsky rejects efforts to construct a *discovery* procedure for grammars and argues that the goal of linguistic theory should instead be the
formulation of an *evaluation* procedure, which would specify which of a
number of alternative grammars is better (51). While claiming that "each
grammar is simply a description of a certain set of utterances" (48), he
also asserts that "a grammar of the language *L* is essentially a theory of

L" and that "our problem is to develop and clarify the criteria for se-
lecting the correct grammar for each language, that is, the correct theory of this language" (49). He maintains that "when we lower our aims to
the development of an evaluation procedure, there remains little motivation for any objection to mixing levels" (57); in turn, then, problems
of segmentation in *took, walked*, etc., can be avoided "by regarding morphology and phonology as two distinct but interdependent levels of representation, related in the grammar by morphophonemic rules" (58).

A different position, however, is taken in *The Sound Pattern of Russian* (1959) by M. Halle, who rejects the dichotomy of morphophonemics and
phonology (13-14):

> In a number of important respects in which it departs from pro-
> cedures that enjoy almost universal acceptance among contemporary
> phonologists, the present description follows methods that are
> characteristic of the work of Edward Sapir. Thus, like the descrip-
> tions of Sapir, the present work does not recognize the need for a
> "phonemic" transcription in addition to a "morphophonemic" tran-
> scription. . . .

While Hockett had said that "For a notation to be phonemic, we require a bi-unique, one-one relation rather than a many-one relation"
(1951:340), Halle not only abandons this condition but charges that it
"is an unwarranted complication which has no place in a scientific description of a language" (1959:24). To support his claim Halle presents
his well-known argument involving the voicing in Russian obstruents (22-
23), whereby he claims to show that the recognition of a level of autonomous phonemics between morphophonemics and phonetics forces one to lose
generalizations that could be captured by combining statements of phonemic alternation and allophonic variation.[8]

While discarding autonomous phonemic representation as being unsci-
entific Halle indicates that a level of morphophonemic representation
must be retained (23):

> Morphophonemic representations cannot be dispensed with in a linguis-
> tic description since they are the means for accounting for ambigui-
> ties due to homophony. E.g., the fact that English [t^{h}æks] ('tacks'
> and 'tax') is ambiguous is normally explained by saying that these
> "phonemically identical" utterances differ morphophonemically.

He takes "morphophonemes" (matrices of distinctive features) as the basic units that "serve to distinguish one morpheme from another" (32). But since Halle makes no distinction between morphophonemics and phonology, the designation 'morphoneme' has no functional significance; the component of morphophonemic rules described by Chomsky 1957a is therefore replaced by a set of simply "phonological" rules (26):

> The final set of rules, the *phonological* rules, takes the transformed terminal strings, which consist entirely of special kinds of segments and boundaries, and completes the assignment of phonetic features to these symbols.

Halle 1962 uses the term 'morphophonemics' only twice, and in these places only incidentally; otherwise the switch to 'phonology' is complete. Chomsky adopts Halle's position and uses the expression 'systematic phonemics' (1964:69-70):

> Systematic phonemics would now generally be called "morphophonemics", in one of the several senses of this term. This terminological innovation is justified if there is a third, intermediate level of systematic representation, more closely related to sound and quite independent of syntactic structure, such as the system of representation now called "phonemic". However . . ., the existence of an additional level is highly dubious, and for this reason I have preferred to keep the older term, modified by "systematic" to avoid confusion.

But in *The Sound Pattern of English* (1968) Chomsky and Halle simply speak of "phonological" rules applying to "phonological" representations (11):

> Other terms that might have been used in place of the terms just proposed are "morphophonemic representation" or "systematic phonemic representation." We have avoided these terms, however, because of the technical meaning they have been given in various theories of sound structure developed in modern linguistics. The term "morphophonemic representation" seems to us appropriate only if there is another linguistically significant level of representation, intermediate in "abstractness" between lexical (phonological) and phonetic and meeting the conditions placed on "phonemic representation" in modern structural linguistics. We feel, however, that the existence of such a level has not been demonstrated and that there are strong reasons to doubt its existence. We will make no further mention of "phonemic analysis" or "phonemes" in this study and will also avoid terms such as "morphophonemic" which imply the existence of a phonemic level. Notice that the issue in this case is not terminological but rather

substantive; the issue is whether the rules of a grammar must be so constrained as to provide, at a certain stage of generation, a system of representation meeting various proposed conditions.

Generative Phonology in Relation to Other Theories

Transformationalist linguists, such as P. Postal (1964) and J. Mc-Cawley (1967), have made a special effort to point out that their understanding of phonology is quite close to that of such scholars as Bloomfield and Sapir.[9] The same view is held by Hockett (1968a:26-27):

> I am inclined to say that, today, the phonological views of the transformationalists are the rather direct descendants of those of Bloomfield, Sapir, and the Prague school, while what they call 'taxonomic phonemics', insofar as it is not purely a straw man, derives from the Bloch-Trager-Hockett notions of the 1940's.

Chomsky (1964:108-9) observes that the arguments of descriptivists against phonology are essentially the same as those they raise against the phonological views of earlier linguists:

> It is interesting to consider the kinds of criticism that have been offered by taxonomic linguists against de Saussure, Sapir and Bloomfield. . . . It is important to observe that these . . . critics have not actually demonstrated that the position of de Saussure, Sapir or Bloomfield is in any way confused. The criticism relies on the assumption that . . . taxonomic phonemics is a significant intermediate level of linguistic structure (so that Sapir and Bloomfield appear to be confusing morphophonemics and taxonomic phonemics in their systematic phonemics). Hence the criticism amounts only to the comment that de Saussure, Sapir and Bloomfield have not developed the level of taxonomic phonemics, but only the levels of systematic phonetics and systematic phonemics. The criticism, then, is only as well-founded as is the status of taxonomic phonemics.

Hockett (1968a:32) grants Chomsky's point but maintains his rejection of the conception of phonology to be seen in Bloomfield[10] and the transformationalists:

> I believe that Trager, Bloch, and I were essentially correct in the early 1940's, as over against Bloomfield then, Pike then or now, or Chomsky and Halle now, in our view of the status of phonology within language design. We were wrong, of course, in accepting without challenge the Saussurean-Bloomfieldian notion of 'letter-sized'

phonemes as the ultimate building-blocks in phonology, but I, at
least, had begun to relinquish that view by the end of the war . . ...

Of course, a distinction between phonology and morphophonemics has
been maintained by many linguists outside the Bloch-Trager-Hockett circle.
Pike (1967:353) criticizes Chomsky's position:

> It seems to me that Chomsky is . . . insensitive to available
> intuitive or psycholinguistic support for the conventional phoneme
> level which he rejects; his model does not call for it, and in his
> reading of Sapir (see Chomsky, 1962, §4.2, p. 532), he senses sup-
> port for the psychological relevance of morphophonemic units but not
> the equally-available support for the relevance of conventional pho-
> nemes. . . . More recent material giving evidence for native reac-
> tion both to a phonemic and to a morphophonemic level are found in
> Gudschinsky [1958:343-45].

S. K. Šaumjan, the initiator of an independent school of generative
grammar in the Soviet Union,[11] also demands that phonology and morphophonemics be recognized as distinct areas (1971:83-84):

> Chomsky, Halle, and certain other linguists draw far-reaching con-
> clusions which lead to their abolishing that essential section of
> the problems studied by modern phonology which is not related to the
> use of phonological means for grammatical purposes. The truth of the
> matter is that in their work these writers replace phonology by mor-
> phophonology, to which they attach the term 'phonology'. The classi-
> cal problems of phonology are declared trivial by these writers.
>   In reality, the situation is as follows. Phonological means
> must, above all, be studied in themselves, i.e., independently of
> how they are used for grammatical purposes. From this standpoint pho-
> nology is a more abstract discipline than morphophonology.[12] In
> fact, if we take phonological means only from the standpoint of their
> diacritic (differentiating) function, independently of their inclu-
> sion in morphemes, we attain a higher level of abstraction than if
> we take phonological means in relation to how they function in mor-
> pheme composition. The aim of morphophonology is to investigate how
> the diacritic potentialities of phonological means are realized for
> grammatical purposes.

Many linguists have tried to steer a middle course between autonomous and systematic phonology—often at the price of inconsistency—or
to achieve a reconciliation between the two.[13] A. A. Hill (1962:10) urges
linguists to tolerate differing understandings of phonology:

I am sure that all three kinds of phoneme [narrow, broad, and sys-
tematic] are valid, useful, and different. A little tolerance all
around would help linguists. To quarrel over which kind of practi-
tioner is alone entitled to the name phoneme, is to quarrel solely
over who owns words. It is a quarrel of the sort that is most common, most useless, and most avoidable.

Concrete versus Abstract Phonology

Criticism of generative phonology came not only from outside but also from among its adherents, and particular scrutiny was directed toward
the "diacritic", or merely differential, use of phonetic features to
avoid the specification of grammatical or lexical information in morphophonemic rules. At the same time the use of phonetically void diacritics[14]
was rejected. These issues, which were grouped together as the problem of
"abstract versus concrete phonology"[15] led to the proposal of various constraints on the sort of underlying representations that would be accepted
in generative grammar. P. Postal (1968:53ff) introduces the "naturalness
condition", according to which, systematic phonemic representations should
differ from phonetic representations "only to the minimum extent necessary
to state the general rules required by alternations, predictable distri-
butions, phonological constraints, etc." (73). P. Kiparsky (1968b) gives
a general discussion of the problem and then presents the "alternation
condition" (10-12):

> Suppose . . . that a grammar contains the phonological rule
>
> $$A \rightarrow B \quad \text{in the context} \_\_\_C.$$
>
> The language has, however, certain instances of C before which the
> change A → B does not take place, but which are in themselves in-
> distinguishable from those C's before which the change does take
> place. In the present theory of generative phonology it is always
> possible to prevent any C from serving as the environment of the
> rule by representing it as an underlying D, where D is a representa-
> tion not otherwise found in the language which differs minimally in
> some way from C. It is then merely necessary to incorporate a late
> rule D → C into the grammar. The obligatory, context-free conver-
> sion of virtual D to phonetic C is an instance of what is here
> termed absolute neutralization. . . .

> Along with such purely diacritic use of phonological features, generative phonology has also allowed the phonological use of diacritic features. By this I mean rules which have the form of phonological rules but operate on diacritic features. . . .
>
> I will propose that the theory of generative phonology must be modified to *exclude* the diacritic use of phonological features, and the phonological use of diacritic features. One of the effects of restricting phonology like this is to enter non-alternating forms in the lexicon in roughly their autonomous phonemic representation. That is, if a form appears in a constant shape, its underlying representation is that shape, except for what can be attributed to low-level automatic processes.

The net effect of such constraints is to produce a considerably less abstract sort of generative phonology, which, in certain respects, lies midway between autonomous phonemics and Bloomfield's morphophonemics. J. McCawley (1967:107) associates this sort of constrained generative phonology with Sapir's approach:

> It should be noted that the constraint that the phonologic inventory be a subset of the phonetic inventory, a constraint which Sapir adhered to virtually without exception, would exclude a large subclass of the possible analyses of generative phonology, namely those in which some underlying contrast is always neutralized phonetically.[16]

Non-Generative Studies on Morphophonemics

An objection similar to Kiparsky's had been raised earlier by E. Stankiewicz (1966:501-02):

> one of the innovations of Halle's [1963] approach lies in defining morphophonemic rules as much as possible with reference to phonological environment and in avoiding reference to morphological conditions. . . . The revamping of morphologically conditioned into phonologically conditioned rules has . . . the disadvantage of obscuring the role of morphophonemic alternations in the grammatical system of a language, a role which was so emphatically pointed out almost a hundred years ago by Baudouin de Courtenay.

His emphasis on the grammatical function of alternations reveals Stankiewicz as a continuator of Trubetzkoy's and Jakobson's views. This and his critical position toward American descriptivist morphophonemics (1967:1895) place him properly in the context of European linguistics.[17]

A notable aspect of Stankiewicz's work is his coordination of morphophonemics with typological studies, which thus carries out a part of Trubetzkoy's original program.[18]

A number of American linguists operate with conceptions of morphophonemics quite distinct from those of either the Chomsky-Halle or the
Bloch-Trager-Hockett groups. Harris (1969:§8.0) defines morphophonemics
as "the change of the phonemic shape of a morpheme"; but this is taken
rather broadly, and other passages suggest that Harris's morphophonemics
serves much the same function as the transformational component for Chomsky:

> From an attempt to isolate the independent elements of sentence con-
> struction, we arrive at two different and separately acting grammat-
> ical systems, which contribute to this construction: a system of
> predicates (with *and, or*) and a system which can be considered an
> extension of morphophonemics (which is change purely of phonemic se-
> quences). The predicate system carries all the objective information
> in the sentence, and the most natural interpretation of its struc-
> ture is that of giving a report. The morphophonemic system is inter-
> pretable as being paraphrastic, and changes at most the speaker's
> or hearer's relation to the report. The grammar of the language as
> a whole is simply the result of these two systems. [§1.0]

> We can say that *by now* has automatically (morphophonemically) pro-
> duced the *have-en*. [§5.3]

> We have to take the elementary ('kernel') sentences or their morpho-
> phonemic sources as a base set . . .. [§7.1]

> The *be* is clearly morphophonemic and not an independent morpheme.
> [§7.4]

H. L. Smith (1967:311) proposes the term 'morphophone' for a cross-
dialectal unit that relates the different phonemic systems encompassed
by an "overall pattern" as presented in Trager and Smith 1951. The unit
allows a word to have a uniform morphophonemic composition in different
dialects even if its phonemic shape varies. This adjustment to a nonhomo-
geneous speech community introduces a new dimension in morphophonemic
theory, but the unit is used much like the older morphophoneme and is
placed "between phoneme and morpheme" in "a three-stratum, twenty-seven
level model for linguistic analysis" (306).

The reference to 'strata' betokens the advent of "stratificational grammar",[19] which had been foreshadowed by works like Trager 1955.[20] The originator and leader of this theoretical movement is S. M. Lamb, who criticizes Chomsky for employing the same phonological components in his underlying forms as in his surface representations. At the root of this criticism lies Lamb's principle that the alternating phonemic units /x/ and /y/ never involve a "process" that converts one to the other, but rather are implementations of a third, fully abstract unit (1966a:39):

> A true stratificational description . . . recognizes a third entity, which is different from both /x/ and /y/, and there is no longer any process. Nothing—neither /x/ nor the underlying entity— ever gets replaced by (or rewritten as) /y/; instead all three entities exist simultaneously.

The underlying entity is called a 'morphon' (cf. 1966b:561), and Lamb indicates that it "corresponds approximately to the classical morphophoneme" (1966a:29). Along with his general rejection of process statements,[21] Lamb criticises the use of rule ordering (1966a:39):

> Another deficiency of process description (even at the highest degree of sophistication) is that it imposes a need for artificial ordering of the rewrite rules; i.e. ordering wnich has no structural significance and is necessary only because of the way rewrite rules operate.

Stratificational grammar may be regarded as the ultimate extension of the IA model, and in fact, Lamb's initial work in this area was done for much the same reasons and at the same time (around 1960) that Hockett sought finally to eradicate the contradictions in the Bloomfieldian conception of the morpheme. Hockett starts from the premise that "Most linguists agree on the existence, or at least on the inescapable utility, of two kinds of basic units in a language: morphemes and phonemes" (1961:29). In terms of these units he presents three assertions constituting "an antilogism—a triad of assertions any two of which imply the negation of the third" (29-30):

(1) *Knife* and *knive-* are the same morpheme.
(2) *Knife* and *knive-* are phonemically different.
(3) A morpheme is composed of phonemes.

Hockett considers the positions corresponding to the different pairs of assertions. Acception (1) and (3) requires a "phoneme" to be reinter-preted as a "pseudo-phoneme" or "morphophoneme" distinct from the "real" phoneme.[22] Accepting (2) and (3) amounts to the allomorph solution, where 'morpheme' is read as 'allomorph' or 'morpheme alternant', and an addi-tional 'morpheme unit' is required. The third combination, of (1) and (3), implies that a morpheme is not composed of phonemes, and this is the pos-sibility Hockett particularly wants to explore. He gives a figure that represents the various positions (32):

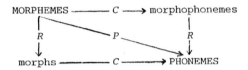

'C' and 'R' mean "(is) composed of (an arrangement of)" and "(is) represented by", respectively (32-33); 'P' denotes a relation that Hockett calls 'is programmed into' or 'is mapped into' (35). While the latter re-lation seems unfamiliar, Hockett asserts that it—together with phonemes and morphemes—constitutes the only reality presented by language; other units—in particular morphs and morphophonemes—are "*artifacts of analy-sis* or *conveniences for description*" (42).[23]

Hockett 1967b is explicitly in the stratificational framework and adopts Lamb's term 'morphon' (§3.0). Employing rigorous mathematical tech-niques Hockett explores three different formats for morphophonemic de-scription (§§3.3-3.10) and finally opts for the rewrite format.[24] He is disturbed, however, that none of the three provide "machinery" for dis-tinguishing "irreducible automatic alternation" from other sorts of al-ternation; the former is explained as follows (§3.10):

> Irreducible automatic alternation differs from all other kinds of alternation in that it is clearly forced on the rest of the lan-guage by the phonological system—by the fact that phonons occur in only certain arrangements, to the exclusion of others: when the rest of the morphophonemics tries, as it were, to generate an illegal ar-ray of phonons, irreducible automatic alternation takes over and en-forces legality.

While retaining the view of autonomous phonology shared by Lamb,[25] Hockett shortly thereafter rejected the rest of stratificational theory.[26] He charges that Lamb, like the transformationalists, "can no longer distinguish between the object of linguistic investigation and the terminological and symbolic machinery we use in that investigation" (1968b:147); while this machinery may have a certain usefulness in itself, Lamb makes the error of attributing linguistic reality to it (1968a:32-33). This criticism reflects a view that is central to Hockett's understanding of morphophonemics and linguistics in general (1967a:221-22):

> One of the most dangerous traps in any of the more complex branches of science . . . is that of confusing one's machinery of analysis with one's object of analysis. One version of this is pandemic in linguistic theory today: almost all theorists take morphophonemes (by one or another name) to be things *in* a language rather than merely part of our equipment for the analysis and description *of* the language. This error is too erudite to be stupid, but it is an error all the same. If the search for economical morphophonemic notations and rules is going to lead us into this trap in the future as it has in the last couple of decades, the price paid for the resulting succinctness of statement is too high.
>
> But if we can keep our wits about us and not be misled by our own cleverness, the trap can be avoided. A correct principal-parts-and-paradigms statement and a correct morphophoneme-and-rule statement subsume the same actual fact of alternation, the former more directly, the latter more succinctly. We ought therefore to be free to use the latter, provided we specify that it is to be understood only as convenient shorthand for the former. As long as this is remembered, there need be no danger.

In "The Yawelmani Basic Verb" (1967a) Hockett first presents a morphophonemic description in rewrite format with ordered rules, but then sketches a principal-parts-and-paradigms statement to cover the same data. He claims, moreover, that the latter format has the advantage of characterizing the mechanism whereby native speakers produce novel utterances— analogy (221).

Since his work within the stratificational framework, Hockett's attention has shifted away from *formal* theories to the "ill-defined" features of language that keep it from being a "rigid" system; he develops this view most extensively in *The State of the Art* (1968a).[27] In keeping with his new orientation, Hockett urges an approach to language free from grammatical preconceptions that impose a structure upon it (1967a:222):

> The grammarian's responsibility . . . is not to find 'the correct'
> solution, for none exists. He should seek the clearest machinery
> of presentation he can, then stand aside and let the language speak
> for itself.

This viewpoint is foreign to most of the linguistic theorizing since Bloomfield, and correspondingly, Hockett calls for a return to earlier methods:

> Before we can once again hope for genuine progress in linguistics,
> we shall have to return virtually to where Bloomfield left us in the
> mid-thirties, and build over again on a more carefully empirical ba-
> sis.[28]

:: :: ::

Linguistics, of course, will not literally return to the methods of Bloomfield any more than it will readopt those of Paul or Pāṇini. Yet it would be foolish to suppose that contemporary theories are in all respects more adequate and insightful than the ones they have replaced. Morphophonemics focuses on perennial questions of language design, and we have seen that many issues controversial today were already raised long ago. Familiarity with the history of linguistics provides not just an appreciation of our heritage but a prerequisite for substantive advances.

NOTES—CHAPTER I

Numbers in parentheses indicate the pages in the text to which the notes refer.

[1] (6) Robins (1967:139) views the bound morpheme as an "analytical creation" and notes that "*morpheme* is generally a technical term, or translated by a technical term, whereas words for *word* are found in a very large number of languages, both written and unwritten . . .."

[2] (7) See below, p. 65.

[3] (7) Cf. Scaglione (1970:74-75): "the two rival schools of analogists and anomalists had finally come to an implicit compromise by settling on the use of multiple paradigms accompanied by exceptions. The Latins had been more successful along this line than the Greeks: Dionysius Thrax had been unable to reduce the verbal patterns to any fewer than thirteen conjugations . . ., a system which Theodore Gaza in the early fifteenth century attempted to reduce to five conjugations. The situation was worse in the realm of nouns, of which Theodosius of Alexandria (end of 4th c. A.D.) codified no fewer than fifty-six declensions . . .."

[4] (7) Also see Robins 1959:119 and 1967:25.

[5] (7) See below, p. 66. Obviously, in speaking of "*the* word-and-paradigm model", one must realize that the actual frameworks employed by Thrax and Priscian only partially resemble the model discussed by Hockett (1954); traditional descriptions of Greek and Latin from modern times *do not* mirror the ancient frameworks.

[6] (8) See the extensive discussion by Balázs (1965), especially p. 284 for Thrax's explanation of the consonantal alternation seen, e.g. in *eípe hópē > eíf' hópē*.

[7] (9) Pāṇini's descriptive techniques, which have long been a topic of special interest among Sanskritists, have recently been dealt with in a series of works, some of which aim beyond the audience of Sanskritists and attempt to present Pāṇini's system in relation to the techniques of modern linguistics. See in particular the works of G. Cardona and J. F. Staal as well as those of W. S. Allen and V. N. Misra.

[8] (10) Misra (1964:746-47) gives an example of a derivation that shows Pāṇini's use of "classifiers".

[9] (11) Cf. Kukenheim (1951:91-92): "Les études grammaticales, chez les Juifs, ne sont pas aussi anciennes que chez les Grecs. Il est même probable que la grammaire de l'hébreu dérive indirectement de Denys de Thrace, dont on connaît des interprétations et des adaptions arméniennes et syriaques, utilisées par les grammariens arabes; ceux-ci, à leur tour, auraient stimulé l'étude de la langue hébraique."

[10] (11) Cf. Fleisch 1961. For medieval Hebrew grammar see Bacher 1892, 1895 and W. Chomsky 1952.

[11] (12) It would be of great interest to see whether the Arab grammarians were able to modify their framework when describing non-Semitic languages. Glazer (1942:106) mentions the Turkish grammar of Abū Ḥayyān (1256-1344) that is "the earliest, or second earliest, grammar of this language still in existence"; one would especially like to know how this work confronts the problem of vowel-harmony, but no studies are available. The treatment by Arab grammarians of suppletive verb stems in Persian might likewise cast light on the flexibility of these investigators, but I have no knowledge of the relevant sources.

[12] (13) Cf. Robins 1967:71; Ó Cuív 1965 and Adams 1970 discuss the school and its terminology.

NOTES—CHAPTER II

[1] (15) An examination of the works discussed in Ch. 2 of Zwirner and Zwirner 1966 would undoubtedly provide a view of the way alternations were described during this period.

[2] (15) *Nikolaj* in Russian; Kruszewski, like Baudouin, was Polish.

[3] (16) The translations quoted from this edition (1972) are by E. Stankiewicz; translations from Baudouin 1963 are by me.

[4] (18) Cf. Jakobson 1971a:396-97 and Koerner 1972b:672-73.

[5] (18) A volume of Kruszewski's selected writings is projected for publication by John Benjamins B. V. (Amsterdam).

[6] (18) Throughout the discussion of Kruszewski and Baudouin I follow their practice of using single or double vertical lines instead of a colon or tilde to indicate alternation.

[7] (19) Kruszewski indicates that Baudouin introduced this term.

[8] (19) See the concise summary of this classification given by Aronson (1968:18-19).

[9] (20) See below, p. 33.

[10] (21) As noted by Koerner (1973a:122), however, H. Paul *did* make a distinction between synchrony and diachrony when he introduced *Laut-wechsel* (for synchronic processes) and *Lautwandel* (for diachronic processes) as technical terms in the 2nd ed. of the *Prinzipien* (1886:§86). Cf. also Koerner 1972c:299. Paul's use of the distinction between these two terms is attributed to Kruszewski by Weinreich et al. (1968:115-16), and Koerner 1972c:299, note 44.

[11] (21) Koerner (1973b:47) reports that "the term 'alternation' is by no means BdC's coinage but in fact, as Baudouin [cf. 1972:148-49; 1895:3] himself acknowledged, a term taken from Saussure's *Mémoire* (p. 12)".

[12] (22) In contrast, Baudouin 1881a gives full credit to Kruszewski. It is extremely difficult to see whether it was Kruszewski or Baudouin who played the larger role in shaping the Kazan School's theory of alternations, and preoccupation with this question appears not to be especially fruitful. Koerner (1972a:74-75, 1972b:674-76, 1973b:45-46) surveys opinions on the problem and himself stresses Kruszewski's contribution, whereas others, e.g. Aronson (1968:18), flatly credit the theory to Baudouin.

[13] (23) The principle of ablaut itself, however, had already been recognized by the Dutch scholar Lambert ten Kate in 1723; cf. Rompelman 1952 and Ising 1956.

[14] (23) In general it is a mistake to suppose that Leskien was a linguist with purely historical interests who contributed nothing to the trend toward structuralism. In the preface to the 1910 edition of his *Handbuch der altbulgarischen (altkirchenslavischen) Sprache* Leskien (1969:v) states that he intended the work as "ein Lehrbuch für eine Einzelsprache in Form einer beschreibenden Grammatik", rather than as a comparison with other Slavic or Indo-European languages. In effect he claims to introduce historical material only in order to explain alternations, e.g. the alternation of *k* with *č* or *c* conditioned by a following *ě*, which depends on the vowel's origin from *$\bar{e}$ or *oi, respectively.

[15] (24) The fact that Baudouin's terminology sounds so modern, however, makes him difficult to read or translate objectively; cf. Koerner 1973b.

[16] (24) The transcription *mož-* is phonemic and *mož̇-*, orthographic.

[17] (24) See below, Ch. 5. Such a passage must have impressed Bloomfield, who refers to Baudouin's *Versuch* in his "Postulates" (1926:§46).

[18] (29) This introduction is now available separately as Stankiewicz 1976.

[19] (29) The former paper first appeared in Polish in *BPTJ* 19.3-34 (1960); the latter was originally published in Italian in *RSlav* 13.3-23 (1965) and in Polish in Kruszewski 1967:x-xxv.

[20] (29) See the discussions by Berezin, Čerepanov, Häusler, Koerner, Leont'ev, Schogt, and Stankiewicz (1964, 1967, 1976). Bogorodic-kij 1931 provides an early account.

[21] (29) Cf. Jakobson 1971b:446ff, Schogt 1966:18, Leont'ev 1966.

[22] (29) Koerner 1972a:72-73 and Stankiewicz 1976:5ff.

[23] (29) Cf. Zimmer 1970.

[24] (30) On the other hand, Jakobson (1971a:414) sees Baudouin's relative isolation in Kazan as providing a better atmosphere for creative innovation than that afforded by the academic centers of western Europe.

[25] (30) Trubetzkoy is aware of this transmission but criticizes Ščerba's 1912 book for spreading erroneous notions about phonology (1975: 349); he expressly dissociates himself from the phonological views of Baudouin and Ščerba.

[26] (33) See above, p. 20.

[27] (33) In contrast, "Projet de terminologie standardisée" (1931) defines morphonology merely as "partie de la phonologie du mot traitant de la structure phonologique des morphèmes" (*TCLP* 4.321), i.e. as the first of Trubetzkoy's three parts.

[28] (34) Cf. Trubetzkoy 1954:5; 1975:259, 319, 488ff.

[29] (34) This appeared as the second part of a projected three-part series on Russian phonology that was to have included contributions by R. Jakobson on word phonology and by S. Karcevskij on syntactic phonology. The original conception of the joint work and Jakobson's reasons for his decision not to have his part published are discussed in the volume of Trubetzkoy's correspondence (1975: xiii, 164, 181, 214-16).

[30] (34) Trubetzkoy uses the terms *Morphemänderung* and *Morphemveränderung* interchangeably (1934:20; cf. 93).

[31] (34) Trubetzkoy abandons the ending -*a* of Ułaszyn's coinage *Morphonema*.

[32] (35) ѱ corresponds to *št* in Bulgarian CS and *šč* in Russian CS but is taken by Trubetzkoy as a unit phoneme in OCS.

[1] (40) Cf. Hockett 1968a, Ch. 3.

[2] (41) Cf. Wolfart 1967 and McQuown 1976. Hanzeli 1969 discusses aspects of this work involving morphophonemics, e.g. "All in all, it may be said that the dictionaries record fairly well the main morphological variants of the nouns; they fail, however, to reflect the pattern of the variations involved. . . . Unable to state [variants'] distribution in a single "grammatical rule," the authors simply listed them in their grammars as possibilities; and the dictionaries, indicating plurals, carried the burden of specifying the type to which each belonged" (89); "As the case with the noun, the verb's morphophonemic changes were too complex for the missionaries to be able to fit them into any pattern permitting a fair degree of predictability" (98).

[3] (42) The expression 'internal change' will be clarified below in the discussion of Sapir.

[4] (42) This does not appear to be a conscious use of 'alternation' as a technical term.

[5] (44) This work actually was completed more than a decade earlier and constituted Sapir's doctoral dissertation.

[6] (44) Kenstowicz (1975:153) points out that "the terms 'organic' and 'primary' versus 'inorganic' and 'secondary' are technical terms for Sapir, referring roughly to the underlying representation versus representations resulting from the application of some phonological rule".

[7] (44) References are to the texts as reprinted in Sapir 1949.

[8] (45) Note Sapir's personal correspondence with Trubetzkoy; see below, fn. 15.

[9] (45) Besides Sapir's own works and Sapir and Swadesh 1939 we have Sapir and Hoijer 1967. In the latter work Hoijer writes, "As a student of Sapir, I have attempted to present the data as he would have done", but in a review R. Stanley (1969:927) declares that "The present monograph bears little similarity to descriptions actually written by Sapir and published during his lifetime". Given Hoijer's stature and background, however, his claim must be treated seriously. Stanley is especially bothered by the multiple base forms for morphemes showing suppletive alternation, and he expects that "the various allomorphs grouped under each base form would be 'phonologically conditioned allomorphs'" (930-31), but this expectation leaves no room for nonsuppletive alternation that constitutes grammatically conditioned phonetic alternation.

[10] (46) Cf. Kenstowicz 1975.

[11] (47) The Bloomfieldian classification is also seen in Ch. 33 of Hockett 1958. In Hockett's opinion the classification of alternations, and especially the definition of automatic alternation, remains a serious problem. See Joshi 1975 and Hockett's comments in a following issue of the same journal.

[12] (48) The original distinction is retained by Hockett (1958:282): "It can thus happen that the base form in some instances is considerably rarer than its replacements. Indeed, in some instances the most conveniently recognized base form never occurs; under these conditions we call it a *theoretical base form*." Thus, Bloomfield writes, "we have no such primary word as *preceive*, but we have the words *precept*, *preceptor*, which are best described as secondary derivatives of a theoretical underlying form *pre-ceive*" (1933:§14.8). In Bloomfield 1939:§4, however, "each morphological element" is to be set up in a "theoretical *basic* form" even when no modification in shape is involved.

[13] (50) See the extensive discussion in Bever 1967.

[14] (51) Cf. Trubetzkoy's letter to R. Jakobson where he refers to Bloomfield as "*moj tovarišč po Lejpcigu* (my colleague in Leipzig)" (1975:335). Jakobson relates that Trubetzkoy, Bloomfield, and L. Tesnière sat together at lectures (personal communication).

[15] (51) Jakobson thinks that Trubetzkoy probably never read Bloomfield's *Language*; he did not read it himself before coming to America (personal communication). Cf. Trubetzkoy's letter to Jakobson from 1935 (1975:335) where the former expresses regret at not having read the book due to his difficulty with English. The same collection of letters demonstrates emphatically, however, that Trubetzkoy and the other members of the Prague Linguistics Circle followed the developments in American linguistics with keen interest. Trubetzkoy was especially impressed by the writings of Sapir, and Jakobson, in Trubetzkoy 1975:vi, speaks of "Sapir's momentous correspondence with [Trubetzkoy] at the beginning of the thirties, in which both linguists pointed out the striking proximity of their approaches to phonology"; this correspondence, sadly, has not survived.

[16] (52) Cf. Bloomfield 1970:351 for the remarks by Hockett: "apparently, when the invitation came to contribute something to this particular volume, he drew on his ongoing and constantly-revised grammar of Menomini, rewriting the section on morphophonemics to stand as an independent article rather than as a connected part of a book. He had not been too happy about the technical term 'morphophonemics' and had rarely used it before 1939 (it does not appear in the 1933 textbook) . . . ."

[17] (52) Except the brief remarks in the letters to Hockett quoted above. Part II, Russian-English, of the *Dictionary of Spoken Russian* (War Department Technical Manual TM 30-944, Washington, D. C., War Department, 1945) contains an unsigned "Grammatical Introduction" which was in fact written by Bloomfield, and this sketch includes §3, "Alternation of Sounds". I have not seen the original edition, but the reprint by Dover Publications, New York (1958) has unfortunate and misleading mistakes which seem to be the "corrections" of an editor.

18 (53) Thus, using 'form' as a technical term Bloomfield writes (1933:
161), "A linguistic form which bears no partial phonetic-semantic
resemblance to any other form, is a *simple* form or *morpheme*. . . .
every complex form is entirely made up, so far as its phonetically definable constituents are concerned, of morphemes. . . .
A morpheme can be described phonetically, since it consists of
one or more phonemes . . .." But 'form' is used nontechnically
in the statement that "Strictly speaking, we should say that the
morpheme in such cases has two (or sometimes, more) different
phonetic forms" (164). It is precisely this equivocation that
allows Bloomfield to skirt the critical question of the relationship between morpheme alternants and morphemes. Huddleston (1972:
339) overlooks Bloomfield's use of 'form' but discovers "some
inconsistency in Bloomfield's use of the term 'alternant'. On
the one hand the different phonetic forms that a morpheme has in
certain environments are said to be its alternants . . .; on the
other hand, in the context of substitution-alternants the meaning
is more or less equivalent to 'alternative to' . . .. Thus we
find him saying of the past-tense for *ran*, a word consisting of
one morpheme, both that *ran* is an alternant of *run* (164) and that
substitution of [ɛ] is an alternant of the plural suffix."

19 (53) Cf. Jakobson 1948:167.

NOTES—CHAPTER IV

1 (56) The dissertation by F. Neisser (1935) was written in Vienna under
Trubetzkoy's direction but does not directly discuss the latter's
theoretical framework or use his terminology for morphonology; cf.
Trubetzkoy 1975:333.

2 (57) But Vachek, after criticizing the psychological basis of Trubetzkoy's definition, says (1966:80) that 'one can redefine the morphoneme as "a set of phonemes functioning in a given phonemic segment of the morpheme in all phonemic implementations of that morpheme"'; also see Vachek 1961:74 for the same point.

3 (58) See below, pp. 73-76.

4 (60) See the descriptive works included in Jakobson 1971. Note that
"Russian Conjugation" follows Bloomfield 1933 and is not properly
Jakobsonian.

5 (60) Ďurovič objects (in Hamm 1967:171) that "es ist nicht begreiflich,
warum das Morphonem ein Prozeß und nicht eine Sache ist".

6 (60) The point is less clear in an English paraphrase by Kuryłowicz
(1968:69): "If we consider the Indo-European ablaut *e* : zero . . .
as morphological, is a contrast like German *Tag* : plur. *Tage* also
to be regarded as morphological *in the same degree*?"

[7] (61) See the discussion of "grammatical prerequisites" below, p. 76.

[8] (62) It should be noted, however, that Jakobson and American linguists do not necessarily coincide in their understanding of 'autonomy'; e.g. the "zero-phoneme" used by Jakobson and Lotz (1949:155) is purely a matter of phonology for them, while American descriptivists would view it as a morphophonemic device.

[9] (62) While Jakobson has said relatively little directly on the subject of morphonology, his influence has been enormous. "Russian Conjugation" led to a long series of articles and dissertations that applied the one-stem system to other Slavic languages, and his students have gone on to explore other aspects of morphophonemics. Thus, the lively discussion of morphophonemic questions now seen in the works of H. Andersen, H. I. Aronson, M. Shapiro, E. Stankiewicz, and D. S. Worth may largely be seen as an extension of Jakobson's theory. See the additional bibliography and discussion in Shapiro 1974.

[10] (62) Cf. Makaev and Kubrjakova 1967 & 1969, Bernštejn 1968, Lopatin and Uluxanov 1969, Red'kin 1969, Čurganova 1973; also see the remarks of S. K. Šaumjan on morphonology and generative grammar below, p. 112.

[11] (63) See below, p. 84.

[12] (64) The papers in Palmer 1970 exemplify the application of prosodic analysis, and Lyons 1962 provides a comparison with morphophonemics. Also see the critique of Firthian linguistics by Langendoen (1968).

[13] (64) I am indebted to K. H. Albrow for discussions on this subject. The analysis of English stems from E. Whitley.

[14] (65) A similar objection is made by D. L. Bolinger (1948) against the "item-and-arrangement" model; cf. Hockett 1968a:29.

[15] (66) See below, p. 118.

NOTES—CHAPTER V

[1] (67) Cf. Joos 1967:96. There need be no objection to the expression 'taxonomic' when used without pejorative overtones. Note that the original conception of "descriptive" linguistics rested on its exclusion of prescriptive and historical considerations.

[2] (67) While the synchronic problem of phonemics versus morphophonemics emerged as an issue in the late 1930's (mainly in discussion between Bloch, Hockett, and Trager), Hockett recently has drawn attention to a contradiction between Bloomfield's synchronic and diachronic phonemics (personal communication): the former is morphophonemic because it takes grammatical considerations into ac-

count, while the latter is based on the neogrammarian assumption
of regular sound change, which in effect denies that grammar has
a bearing on phonemics; consequently, Bloomfield's synchronic and
diachronic phonemics are based on different units.

3 (70) See below, p. 113.

4 (71) Cf. the letter of Trubetzkoy (1975:349) to Jakobson from 1935: "In
the December issue of *Language* there is an article by Trager on
the phonemes of Russian. In general it's all nonsense and factu-
ally wrong, but one shouldn't simply abuse him. He (incidentally,
like Swadesh [1934] in the same volume) apparently is trying to be
"ours", uses our terminology, etc. On the whole in morphonology I
was able to avoid arguing with anyone because nobody had written
about it . . .."

5 (72) Compare Hockett's understanding of 'preliminary normalization'
(1947b:§§4-7).

6 (73) Note how closely this parallels the passages in Harris 1951a:219
discussed below, p. 86.

7 (73) Chao (p. 54): "It is not necessary to take serious exception to
anyone's transcription so long as it is self-consistent and its
interpretation is clear to the extent it is meant for, and so long
as it does not claim unique correctness to the exclusion of other
possible treatments. Usage may in time become unified, but problems will always vary. Our motto must be: Write, and let write!"

8 (75) The philosophical issues involved here are subtle. The assertion
that water boils at 100 degrees Celsius under standard pressure is
a tautology but has an empirical basis and may convey information.

9 (77) Bloch 1948:5 is more apologetic than Hockett: "The basic assumptions that underlie phonemics, we believe, can be stated without
any mention of mind and meaning; but meaning, at least, is so obviously useful as a shortcut in the investigation of phonemic
structure—one might almost say, so inescapable—that any linguist
who refused to employ it would be very largely wasting his time."

10 (77) The term stems from Hockett 1942:§6.

11 (78) Personal communication; Pike (in a personal communication) rejects
Hockett's interpretation, however.

12 (81) Hockett 1968a:28 shows a lapse of memory.

13 (82) Bloch also proposes a notational convention that is sometimes ob-
served in the literature (1947:§3.1): "Alternants whose choice
depends on the last preceding phoneme (automatic alternants) are
connected by a curve (∿); alternants whose choice depends not on
a phonemic feature but on the base itself (non-automatic alternants) are separated by a semicolon."

[14] (82) Wells stresses (114) that Emeneau 1944:5 uses 'automatic' in a
different sense in speaking of changes that are predictable in
terms of morphophonemes. Note that Bloch 1941:283 uses 'automatic
alternation' for 'subphonemic variation'; also see above, fn. 13.
Hockett rejects Wells's definition (personal communication) and
understands automatic alternation as involving the replacement
of a base form by one or more other alternants "under specific
conditions where, otherwise, there would be an arrangement of
phonemes contrary to the phonemic pattern of the language" (1958:
279-80); cf. Bloomfield's definition above, p. 47.

[15] (82) See above, Ch. II, fn. 29; cf. Karcevskij 1931.

[16] (82) The same view is developed in Harris 1945a:285.

[17] (82) Cf. Hockett (1954:§2.10): "The statement of shapes, alternations,
and conditions of alternation describes the *morphophonemic pattern* of the language."

[18] (84) But Hockett also briefly considers a definition in terms of 'hab-
it' in the same period (1956:815): [Morphophonemics is] "the phonemic shapes which represent morphemes and larger forms, and the
habits of alternation among these shapes . . ... Morphophonemics
is thus a set of habits bridging between grammar and phonology."

[19] (84) Note that 'representation' is a technical term having nothing to
do with transcription; cf. Hockett (1958:135): "For the relationship of a morpheme to any of its phonemic shapes, we use the
phrase *is represented by* . . .."

[20] (85) Compare this with B. L. Whorf (1942), who recognizes a separate
morphophonemic plane between those of phonemics and morphology;
he speaks of 'the morphophonemic plane in which the "phonemes"
of the previous level appear combined into "morphemes"' (249).

[21] (85) Recall that 'alternation' encompasses only relations of this sort
for Trubetzkoy; see above, p. 35.

[22] (86) Not even in Harris 1951a.

[23] (86) See below, p. 97.

[24] (86) See above, p. 31.

[25] (87) See above, p. 50.

[26] (88) This passage conflicts with Hockett's later understanding of 'automatic', however; see above, fn. 14.

[27] (89) One also senses a similarity between this issue and the more recent question of "abstract" versus "concrete" generative phonology; see below, p. 113.

[28] (90) Harris (1944a: fn. 1) acknowledges his debt to Jakobson for principles concerning distinctive features.

[29] (90) See above, pp. 111-12.

[30] (90) One should also bear in mind that the distributionally-oriented phonemics of Trager and Smith 1951, especially the use of /h/ as a semivowel, struck many linguists as highly abstract and remote from phonetics. This development in turn helped pave the way for the much more abstract phonological representations of generative phonology.

[31] (90) See Bloomfield 1939:§4 quoted above, p. 49.

[32] (91) But see the remarks (1958:466) by Hockett on this particular example, which is invalid.

[33] (92) See above, p. 25.

[34] (93) See the extensive discussion by R. Huddleston (1972). The remarks that follow here do not deal with the crucial issue of the status of *took* as monomorphemic or bimorphemic (cf. Bloch 1947:§1.2), but this problem raises the central questions of *morphological* theory and thus exceeds the intended scope of this book. However, readers should keep in mind the distinction between (1) a process model that e.g. derives the past tense form *took* from the base *take* by vowel change, and (2) a process model that uses rules to derive phonemic transcriptions of actually pronounced forms from abstract representations of the constituent morphological elements; the latter type may also be construed as IA in a narrower sense.

[35] (95) Cf. Pike (1967:556): 'Harris [1944b:203-5] seemed to imply that, in general, modern linguistics should preferably not imply "primacy of the base" or a "motion analogy" of process but deal with distribution. Soon after the appearance of this article, the general trend of American linguistics for the next decade was to use item-and-arrangement statements—with process statements carrying low prestige. Nida, for example, changed largely from process to item-and-arrangement (allomorphic-item-in-distribution) statement between the 1946 and 1949 editions of his *Morphology*.' Pike also claims (557) that, in moving toward IA, linguistics was "moving contrary to the general stream of the philosphy of science".

[36] (96) Besides Harris 1947, which is based on this material, see the review by Hockett (1948a).

[37] (96) P. Newman (1968:508) tailors the passage to fit his claim that Harris was advocating IA: 'Harris . . . suggested that a preferable [Harris said 'possible'] approach would be "to speak directly in terms of the *observable* morphemes and phonemes" (1945:286)'; see the quotation from Pike above, fn. 35, with the same distortion of Harris's stated view.

[38] (96) But one should recall the distinction made above in fn. 34 between two different kinds of "process" model; it is the second type that is reducible to IA.

39 (97) Harris, however, had already used such lists and other devices of *Methods* in his Hebrew sketch of 1941. One should also note the similarity of Harris's list format to the rewrite rules of generative grammar.

40 (97) Cf. Huddleston 1972:335-36.

41 (98) This work is strongly oriented toward the traditional sort of IP in both of its editions, e.g. Nida (1949:200): "Under the subdivisions of phonologically and morphologically definable environments the different allomorphic alternations should be classified [in the morphophonemic section of a slip file], in so far as they can be, under phonological processes, e.g. assimilation, dissimilation, reduction of clusters, loss of final vowels, palatalization, and nasalization."

42 (98) See Hockett 1968a:29 for a discussion of misinterpretations by other linguists.

43 (100) Hockett would agree with Harris 1954:161, however: 'We cannot directly investigate the rules of "the language" via some system of habits or some neurological machine that generates all the utterances of the language. We have to investigate some actual corpus of utterances, and derive therefrom such regularities as would have generated these utterances—and would presumably generate other utterances of the language than the ones in our corpus.'

44 (100) Cf. Householder 1952 and Hockett 1948b

NOTES—CHAPTER VI

1 (103) Hockett 1968a:29 indicates, however, that this article was written already in 1950.

2 (103) Also see Carnap 1937; one can find a certain irony in the fact that Carnap's logical syntax exhibits both the positivistic, antimentalistic position associated with Bloomfiedian linguistics as well as syntactic techniques used by transformationalist linguists.

3 (106) In relation to the thesis Chomsky says that "In the light of more recent work, the grammar . . . would have to be modified in many respects, but the conclusion concerning ordering, so it appears, would, if anything, be strengthened" (1964:71).

4 (106) Compare this, especially in regard to the second and third points, with the discussion in P. Kiparsky 1968a: Kiparsky says that rules *A* and *B* are (1) in a *feeding* order if "the application of *A* creates the representations to which *B* is applicable" (p. 196) and (2) in a *bleeding* order if "*A* removes representations to which *B* would otherwise apply" (198); Kiparsky then hypothesizes that "Feeding order tends to be maximized" (197) and that "Bleeding order tends to be minimized" (199) in the "internalized grammars" of speakers. Also see Chafe 1968.

[5] (106) Cf. Chomsky 1964:70.

[6] (107) The mathematical principle of transitivity makes it unnecessary to show that R_i precedes R_k if it has been established that R_i precedes R_j and that R_j precedes R_k.

[7] (107) Justification of the individual ordering constraints occupies pp. 51-58; pp. 59-69 present sample morphophonemic derivations.

[8] (109) Lamb 1966b:544-47 rejects Halle's argument because of the auton- omous phonemic analysis it proposes and then attacks; Hockett en- dorses Lamb's discussion (personal communication). Chomsky 1966: 50-51 and Postal 1968:39ff in turn attack Lamb's analysis.

[9] (111) A series of recent works has reexamined earlier American writing on phonemics and morphophonemics for its bearing on current the- oretical issues; cf. e.g. Bever 1967, Lightner 1970, and Kensto- wicz 1975.

[10] (111) Note Hockett's anecdote in Bloomfield (1970:541): 'J M. Cowan has reminded me (I had forgotten it) that in the summer of 1938 or 1939, at Ann Arbor, during a public discussion, I said "The trouble with you, Mr. Bloomfield, is that you don't believe in the phonemic principle!" This must have been virtually our first meeting; I tell the story, with some chagrin, only because [Bloomfield's] action in rising above the remark was so indica- tive of his stature.' Hockett indicates that his remark probably centered around Bloomfield's use of word boundaries in phonemics (personal communication).

[11] (112) Generative phonology in Germany, however, has been strongly in- fluenced by American work; see the bibliography in Clément and Grünig 1972.

[12] (112) The reader should give special consideration to this claim. It could be that Bloomfield found his "morphophonemicized" phonemes to be more tangible than the units one is forced to recognize when working with criteria of strictly autonomous phonemic anal- ysis.

[13] (112) A notable attempt at the latter is provided by Schane 1971. Schane 1966, like many other generative works, retains the term 'morphophonemics'.

[14] (113) Such as Bloomfield's use of capital 'N' versus small 'n' (see above, p. 50); Kisseberth 1969:252ff directs the same criticism against the "effect morphophonemes" used in Hockett 1967a:209. Also see Bloomfield 1945, Voegelin 1947:246, Hall 1948:19, Hamp 1951:231-32, and Gibson 1956:§3.2.2, §3.5.2.

[15] (113) See Hyman 1970 and Schane 1973; the recent literature on this
             subject is quite large.

[16] (114) McCawley notes, however, that the principle is violated in Sapir
             and Swadesh 1939.

[17] (114) See above, Ch. IV, fn. 9.

[18] (115) See above, p. 33.

[19] (116) Cf. Roberts 1970 and Huddleston 1972 for stratificational mor-
             phophonemics.

[20] (116) The theme of Trager's 1955 paper, the morphophonemics of the
             French verb, has been a favorite "testing ground" for morphopho-
             nemic techniques. Trager's 1944 article on the same subject pro-
             voked a reply from Bloomfield (1945) which rejected Trager's
             cumbersome morphophonemic apparatus and proposed an alternative
             description. Hall 1948 and Schane 1966 show additional possibil-
             ities.

[21] (116) Lamb charges that "the process or rewriting formulation . . .
             crept into morphophonemic description from diachronic linguis-
             tics" (1966b:551).

[22] (117) Or gives morphophonemics without phonemics, so that 'phoneme'
             can be read as 'systematic phoneme'.

[23] (117) Hockett (1961:29): "Morphophonemes are pseudo-phonemes· so devised
             that morphemes could be said to compose them. Morphs are pseudo-
             morphemes so devised that phonemes could be said to compose them."

[24] (117) Also note Hockett's remark that "Outside of syntax, ordered rules
             are a wonderfully clarifying device in morphophonemics" (1968a:
             34).

[25] (118) Cf. Hockett 1968a:32.

[26] (118) Cf. Hockett (1968b:153): "So in the end, how many strata do we
             need? Not Lamb's current eleven or six. Not my two of 1961. Not
             even just one. None at all. The stratificational view was an er-
             ror from the outset."

[27] (118) See, Hockett 1973 for his recent views on generative phonology
             and the status of morphophonemes.

[28] (119) *Current Anthropology* 9.128 (1968).

ABBREVIATIONS

IJAL   *International Journal of American Linguistics*

IUZ   *Izvestija i učenye zapiski imp. kazanskogo universiteta*

JAOS   *Journal of the American Oriental Society*

Lg   *Language*

RFV   *Russkij filologičeskij vestnik*

RIL   *Readings in Linguistics*, ed. by M. Joos, Chicago, [4]1967.

SIL   *Studies in Linguistics*

TCLP   *Travaux du Cercle linguistique de Prague*

TPS   *Transactions of the Philological Society*

VJ   *Voprosy jazykoznanija*

REFERENCES

Adams, G. B. 1970. "Grammatical Analysis and Terminology in the Irish Bardic Schools". *Folia Linguistica* 4.157-66.

Akhmanova, O. 1971. *Phonology, Morphonology, Morphology*. The Hague and Paris: Mouton.

Albrow, K. H. 1962. "The Phonology of the Personal Forms of the Verb in Russian". *Archivum Linguisticum* 14.146-56.

Allen, W. S. 1953. *Phonetics in Ancient India*. London, New York, Toronto.

_____. 1955. "Zero and Pāṇini". *Indian Linguistics* 16.106-13.

Andersen, H. 1969. "A Study in Diachronic Morphophonemics: The Ukrainian Prefixes". *Lg* 45.807-30.

Aronson, H. I. 1968. *Bulgarian Inflectional Morphology*. The Hague: Mouton.

Austerlitz, R. 1967. "The Distributional Identification of Finnish Morphophonemes". *Lg* 43.20-33.

Avanesov, R. I. 1955. "Kratčajšaja zvukovaja edinica v sostave slova i morfemy", *Voprosy grammatičeskogo stroja*, 113-39. Moscow. (Repr. in Avanesov 1956b.)

_____. 1956a. "O trex tipax naučno-lingvističeskix transkripcij (v svjazi s voprosami teorii fonem)". *Slavia* 25.347-71. (Also in Avanesov 1956b.)

_____. 1956b. *Fonetika sovremennogo russkogo literaturnogo jazyka*. Moscow.

Axvlediani, V. G. 1966. *Fonetičeskij traktat Avicenny*. Tbilisi: Izd. "Mecniereba".

Bacher, W. 1892. *Die hebräische Sprachwissenschaft vom 10. bis zum 16. Jahrhundert*. Trier. (Repr. 1974 together with Bacher 1895, Amsterdam: John Benjamins B. V.)

_____. 1895. *Anfänge der hebräischen Grammatik*. Leipzig. (Repr. 1974 together with Bacher 1892.)

Balázs, J. 1965. "The Forerunners of Structural Prosodic Analysis and Phonemics". *Acta linguistica Academiae scientiarum Hungaricae* 15.229-to 287.

Baudouin de Courtenay, J. 1881a. Review of Kruszewski 1881a. *IUZ* 3.18-20.

_____. 1883. Review of Kruszewski 1883. *IUZ* 2.233-34.

_____. 1888-89. "Mikołaj Kruszewski, jego życie i prace naukowe". *Prace filologiczne* 2.837-49, 3.116-75. (Russ. tr. in Baudouin de Courtenay 1963 I:146-202.)

_____. 1894. *Próba teorji alternacyj fonetycznych*. Cracow.

_____. 1895. *Versuch einer Theorie phonetischer Alternationen: Ein Kapitel aus der Psychophonetik*. Strassburg: Trübner.

_____. 1963. *Izbrannye trudy po obščemu jazykoznaniju*, 2 vols., comp. by V. P. Grigor'ev and A. A. Leont'ev. Moscow: Izd. AN SSSR.

_____. 1972. *A Baudouin de Courtenay Anthology*, tr. and ed. with an intro. by E. Stankiewicz. Bloomington and London: Indiana U. P.

Bazell, C. E. 1938. "Archiphoneme and Phonomorpheme". *Modern Language Notes* 53.363-66.

_____. 1956. "Three Conceptions of Phonological Neutralization", *For Roman Jakobson*, comp. by M. Halle, 25-30. The Hague: Mouton.

Berezin, F. M. 1968. *Očerki po istorii jazykoznanija v Rossii: Konec XIX. —načalo XX. v.* Moscow: Izd. "Nauka".

Beeston, A. F. L. 1970. *The Arabic Language Today*. London: Hutchinson University Library.

Bernštejn, S. B. 1968. "Vvedenie v slavjanskuju morfonologiju". *VJ* 4.43-59.

Bever, T. G. 1967. *Leonard Bloomfield and the Phonology of the Menomini Language*. Ph.D. diss., M. I. T.

Bloch, B. 1941. "Phonemic Overlapping". *American Speech* 16.278-84. (Repr. in *RIL*, 93-96.)

_____. 1947. "English Verb Inflection". *Lg* 23.399-418. (Repr. in *RIL*, 243-54.)

_____. 1948. "A Set of Postulates for Phonemic Analysis". *Lg* 24.3-46.

_____. 1950. "Studies in Colloquial Japanese IV: Phonemics". *Lg* 26.86-125.

Bloomfield, L. 1914. *An Introduction to the Study of Language*. New York: Holt.

_____. 1917. *Tagalog Texts with Grammatical Analysis* (= *University of Illinois Studies in Language and Literature*, Vol. 3, Nos. 2-4.)

_____. 1922. Review of Sapir 1921. *The Classical Weekly* 15.142-43. (Repr. in Bloomfield 1970:91-94.)

_____. 1925. "Notes on the Fox Language" (Sections 1-3). *IJAL* 3.219-32.

Bloomfield, L. 1926. "A Set of Postulates for the Science of Language".
Lg 2.153-64. (Repr. in *RIL*, 26-31, and Bloomfield 1970:128-38.)

_____. 1927. "On Some Rules of Pāṇini". *JAOS* 47.61-70. (Repr. in
Bloomfield 1970:157-65.)

_____. 1929. Review of Liebich. *Lg* 5.267-75. (Repr. in Bloomfield
1970:219-26.)

_____. 1933. *Language.* New York: Holt.

_____. 1939. "Menomini Morphophonemics". *TCLP* 8.105-15. (Repr. in
Bloomfield 1970:351-62.)

_____. 1945. "On Describing Inflection". *Monatshefte für deutschen
Unterricht* 37.4/5.8-13.

_____. 1958. *Eastern Ojibwa: Grammatical Sketch, Texts, and Word List.*
Ann Arbor: U. of Michigan Press.

_____. 1962. *The Menomini Language.* New Haven and London: Yale U. P.

_____. 1970. *A Leonard Bloomfield Anthology,* ed. by C. F. Hockett.
Bloomington and London: Indiana U. P.

Boas, F. 1889. "On Alternating Sounds". *American Anthropologist* 2.47-53.

_____. 1911. "Tsimshian", "Kwakiutl", "Chinook", and "Siouan (Dakota)",
the last with J. R. Swanton, *Handbook of American Indian Languages,*
Part 1, ed. by F. Boas (= Bureau of American Ethnology, *Bulletin* 40.)

_____. 1917. *Grammatical Notes on the Language of the Tlingit Indians*
(= *Anthropological Publications of the University Museum of the University of Philadelphia,* Vol. 8, No. 1.) Philadelphia.

_____, and E. Deloria. 1941. *Dakota Grammar* (= *Memoirs of the National
Academy of Sciences,* Vol. 23, Pt. 2.) Washington: U.S. Gov. Printing
Office.

_____. 1947. *Kwakiutl Grammar with a Glossary of the Suffixes,* ed. by
H. B. Yampolsky with the collaboration of Z. S. Harris (= *Transactions
of the American Philosophical Society,* New Series, Vol. 37, Pt. 3,
201-377.)

Bogorodickij, V. 1931. "Kazanskij period professorskoj dejatel'nosti I.
A. Boduèna de Kurtenè (1875-1883 g.)". *Prace filologiczne* 15, Fasc. 2,
465-79.

Bolinger, D. L. 1948. "On Defining the Morpheme". *Word* 4.18-23.

Brugmann, K. 1882. Review of Kruszewski 1881b. *Literarisches Centralblatt*
12.400-1.

Bulygina, T. V. 1964. "Pražskaja lingvističeskaja škola", *Osnovnye naprav-
lenija strukturalizma.* Moscow: AN SSSR, Institut jazykoznanija.

Cardona, G. 1965. "On Pāṇini's Morphophonemic Principles". *Lg* 41.225-38.

_____. 1967. "Negations in Pāṇinian Rules". *Lg* 43.34-56.

_____. 1968. Review of Misra 1966. *Lg* 44.643-49.

_____. 1969. *Studies in Indian Grammarians I: The Method of Description Reflected in the Śivasūtras* (= *Transactions of the American Philosophical Society*, 59:1.) Philadelphia.

Carnap, R. 1928. *Der Logische Aufbau der Sprache*. Berlin.

_____. 1935. *Philosophy and Logical Syntax*. London.

_____. 1937. *The Logical Syntax of Language*. London.

Chafe, W. L. 1968. "The Ordering of Phonological Rules". *IJAL* 34.115-36.

Chao, Y.-R. 1934. "The Non-Uniqueness of Phonemic Solutions of Phonetic Systems". *Bulletin of the Institute of History and Philology*, Academia Sinica, Vol. 4, Pt. 4, 363-97. (Repr. in *RIL*, 38-54.)

Čerepanov, M. V. 1969. *Otraženie principov Kazanskoj školy v issledovanijax N. V. Kruševskogo*. Saratov: Saratovskij gos. ped. institut.

Chomsky, N. 1951. *Morphophonemics of Modern Hebrew*. M.A. thesis, U. of Pennsylvania.

_____. 1957a. *Syntactic Structures*. The Hague: Mouton.

_____. 1957b. Review of Hockett 1955. *IJAL* 23.223-34.

_____. 1962. "The Logical Basis of Linguistic Theory", *Preprints of the Ninth International Congress of Linguists*, 509-74.

_____. 1964. *Current Issues in Linguistic Theory*. The Hague: Mouton.

_____. 1966. "Topics in the Theory of Generative Grammar", *Current Trends in Linguistics*, Vol. 3: *Theoretical Foundations*, ed. by T. A. Sebeok. The Hague: Mouton.

_____, and M. Halle. 1968. *The Sound Pattern of English*. New York, Evanston, and London: Harper and Row.

_____, M. Halle, and F. Lukoff. 1956. "On Accent and Juncture in English", *For Roman Jakobson*, comp. by M. Halle, 65-80. The Hague: Mouton.

Chomsky, W. 1952. *David Ḳimḥi's Hebrew Grammar (Mikhlol)*. New York.

Čurganova, V. G. 1973. *Očerk russkoj morfonologii*. Moscow.

Clément, D., and B. Grünig. 1972. *La grammaire générative en pays de langue allemande* (= *Langages* 26.) Paris.

Cohen, M. 1939. "Catégories de mots et phonologie". *TCLP* 8.36-42.

Ďurovič, L. 1967. "Das Problem der Morphonologie", *To Honor Roman Jakobson* I, 556-68. The Hague: Mouton.

Emeneau, M. B. 1944. *Kota Texts*, Pt. 1. Berkeley and Los Angeles: U. of California Press.

Firth, J. R. 1934. "The Word 'Phoneme'". *Le Maître Phonétique* 46. (Repr. in Firth 1957a.)

_____. 1935. "The Use and Distribution of Certain English Sounds". *English Studies* 17.8-18. (Repr. in Firth 1957a.)

_____. 1936. "Alphabets and Phonology in India and Burma". *Bulletin of the School of Oriental Studies* 8.517-46. (Repr. in Firth 1957a.)

_____. 1948. "Sounds and Prosodies". *TPS* 1948.127-52. (Repr. in Firth 1957a and Palmer 1970.)

_____. 1950. "Personality and Language in Society". *The Sociological Review* 42.37-52. (Repr. in Firth 1957a.)

_____. 1951. "General Linguistics and Descriptive Grammar". *TPS* 1951. 69-87. (Repr. in Firth 1957a.)

_____. 1957a. *Papers in Linguistics 1934-1951*. London: Oxford U. P.

_____. 1957b. "A Synopsis of Linguistic Theory 1930-1955", *Studies in Linguistic Analysis*, 1-32. Oxford: Basil Blackwell. (Repr. in Firth 1968a.)

_____. 1968a. *Selected Papers of J. R. Firth,* ed. by F. R. Palmer. Bloomington and London: Indiana U. P.   .

_____. 1968b. "A New Approach to Grammar", Firth 1968a:114-25.

Fleisch, H. 1961. *Traité de philologie arabe.* Vol. 1 (= *Recherches* publiées sous la direction de l'Institut de Lettres Orientales des Beyrouth, 16.) Beyrouth: Impr. Catholique.

Garvin, P. L. 1962. "Ponapean Morphophonemics". *Phonetica* 8.115-27.

Gibson, L. F. 1956. "Pame (Otomi) Phonemics and Morphophonemics". *IJAL* 22.242-65.

Glazer, S. 1942. "A Noteworthy Passage from an Arab Grammatical Text". *JAOS* 62.106-8.

Gleason, H. A. 1965. *Linguistics and English Grammar*. New York.

Goodman, N. 1943. "Simplicity of Ideas". *Journal of Symbolic Logic* 8.107-21.

Gudschinsky, S. C. 1958. "Native Reactions to Tones and Words in Mazatec". *Word* 14.338-45.

Häusler, F. 1968. *Das Problem Phonetik und Phonologie bei Baudouin de Courtenay und in seiner Nachfolge.* Halle (Saale): Niemeyer.

Hall, R. A., Jr. 1948. *Structural Sketches 1: French (= Language Monographs,* 24.) Baltimore, Md.: Linguistic Society of America.

_____. 1964. *Introductory Linguistics*. Philadelphia: Clinton Books.

Halle, M. 1959. *The Sound Pattern of Russian*. The Hague: Mouton.

_____. 1962. "Phonology in Generative Grammar". *Word* 18.54-72.

Halle, M. 1963. "O pravilax russkogo sprjaženija", *American Contributions to the Fifth International Congress of Slavists* I, 113-32. The Hague: Mouton.

Hamm, J., ed. 1967. *Phonologie der Gegenwart: Vorträge und Diskussionen anläßlich der internationalen Phonologie-Tagung in Wien 30.VIII.-3.IX. 1966*. Graz, Wien, Köln: Herman Böhlaus Nachf.

Hamp, E. P. 1951. "Morphophonemes of the Keltic Mutations". *Lg* 27.230-47.

Hanzeli, V. E. 1969. *Missionary Linguistics in New France: A Study of Seventeenth- and Eighteenth-Century Descriptions of American Indian Languages*. The Hague: Mouton.

Harris, Z. S. 1941a. "The Linguistic Structure of Hebrew". *JAOS* 61.143-67.

_____. 1941b. Review of Trubetzkoy 1939. *Lg* 17. 345-49.

_____. 1942. "Morpheme Alternants in Linguistic Analysis". *Lg* 18.169-80. (Repr. in *RIL*, 109-15, and in Harris 1970:78-90.)

_____. 1944a. "Simultaneous Components in Phonology". *Lg* 20.181-205. (Repr. in *RIL*, 124-38, and in Harris 1970:3-31.)

_____. 1944b. "Yokuts Structure and Newman's Grammar". *IJAL* 10.196-211. (Repr. in Harris 1970:188-208.)

_____. 1945a. Review of Emeneau 1944. *Lg* 21.283-89. (Repr. in Harris 1970:209-16.)

_____. 1945b. "Navaho Phonology and Hoijer's Analysis". *IJAL* 11.239-46. (Repr. in Harris 1970:177-87.)

_____. 1946. "From Morpheme to Utterance". *Lg* 22.161-83. (Repr. in *RIL*, 142-53, and Harris 1970:100-25.)

_____. 1947. "Structural Restatements: I and II". *IJAL* 13.47-58, 175-86. (Repr. in Harris 1970:217-34, 34-50.)

_____. 1951a. *Methods in Structural Linguistics*. Chicago: U. of Chicago Press. (Repr. 1960 with the title *Structural Linguistics*.)

_____. 1951b. Review of Sapir 1949. *Lg* 27.288-332. (Repr. in Harris 1970:712-64.)

_____. 1954. "Distributional Structure". *Word* 10.146-62. (Repr. in Harris 1970:775-794.)

_____. 1969. *The Two Systems of Grammar: Report and Paraphrase* (= *Transformation and Discourse Analysis Papers*, 79.) (Repr. in Harris 1970:612-692.)

_____. 1970. *Papers in Structural and Transformational Linguistics*. Dordrecht: Reidel.

Haslev, M. 1972. *Morfofonemikk: Synkrone og diakrone aspekter*. Oslo: Universitätsforlaget

Haugen, E. 1951. "Directions in Modern Linguistics". *Lg* 27.211-22. (Repr. in *RIL*, 357-63.)

Hill, A. A. 1962. "Various Kinds of Phonemes". *SIL* 16.3-10.

Hjelmslev, L. 1939. "Note sur les oppositions supprimables". *TCLP* 8.51-57.

Hockett, C. F. 1940. Review of Boas, *Handbook*, Pt. 3. *Lg* 16.54-57.

_____. 1942a. "A System of Descriptive Phonology". *Lg* 18.3-21. (Repr. in *RIL*, 97-108.)

_____. 1942b. "English Verb Inflection". *SIL* 1.1-8.

_____. 1947a. Review of Nida 1946. *Lg* 23.273-85.

_____. 1947b. "Problems of Morphemic Analysis". *Lg* 23.321-43. (Repr. in *RIL*, 229-42.)

_____. 1948a. Review of Hoijer 1946. *Lg* 24.183-88.

_____. 1948b. "A Note on 'Structure'". *IJAL* 14.269-71. (Repr. in *RIL*, 279-80.)

_____. 1948c. "Implications of Bloomfield's Algonquian Studies". *Lg* 24.117-31. (Repr. in *RIL*, 281-89.)

_____. 1948d. "Potawatomi". *IJAL* 14.1-10, 63-73, 139-49, 213-25.

_____. 1949. "Two Fundamental Problems in Phonemics". *SIL* 7.29-51.

_____. 1950. "Peiping Morphophonemics". *Lg* 26.63-85. (Repr. in *RIL*, 315-28.)

_____. 1951. Review of Martinet 1949a. *Lg* 27.333-42.

_____. 1954. "Two Models of Grammatical Description". *Word* 10.210-34. (Repr. in *RIL*, 386-99.)

_____. 1955. *A Manual of Phonology* (= *Indiana University Publications in Anthropology and Linguistics, Memoir* 11.) Baltimore.

_____. 1956. Review of Martin 1954. *Lg* 32.814-19.

_____. 1958. *A Course in Modern Linguistics.*New York: MacMillan.

_____. 1961. "Linguistic Elements and their Relations". *Lg* 37.29-53.

_____. 1967a. "The Yawelmani Basic Verb". *Lg* 43.208-22.

_____. 1967b. *Language, Mathematics, and Linguistics*. The Hague: Mouton.

_____. 1968a. *The State of the Art*. The Hague: Mouton.

_____. 1968b. Review of Lamb 1966a. *IJAL* 34.145-53.

_____. 1973. "Yokuts as Testing-Ground for Linguistic Methods". *IJAL* 39.63-79.

Hoenigswald, H. M. 1944. "Internal Reconstruction". *SIL* 2.78-87.

_____. 1946. "Sound Change and Linguistic Structure". *Lg* 22.138-43. (Repr. in *RIL*, 139-41.)

_____. 1960. *Language Change and Linguistic Reconstruction*. Chicago: U. of Chicago Press.

Hoijer, H. 1945. *Navaho Phonology* (= *University of New Mexico Publications in Anthropology*, 1.) Albuquerque.

_____, et al. 1946. *Linguistic Structures of Native America* (= *Viking Fund Publications in Anthropology*, 6.) New York.

Householder, F. W., Jr. 1952. Review of Harris 1951a. *IJAL* 18.260-68.

Huddleston, R. 1972. "The Development of a Non-Process Model in American Structural Linguistics". *Lingua* 30.333-84.

Hyman, L. M. 1970. "How Concrete is Phonology". *Lg* 46.58-76.

Ising, E. 1956. "Die Begriffe 'Umlaut' und 'Ablaut' in der Terminologie der frühen deutschsprachigen Grammatik". *Sitzungsberichte der Deutschen Akademie der Wissenschaften zu Berlin*, Jahrgang 1955, No. 3, 21-45.

Jakobson, R. 1929. *Remarques sur l'évolution phonologique du russe comparée à celle des autres langues slaves* (= *TCLP* 2.)

_____. 1948. "Russian Conjugation". *Word* 4.155-67.

_____. 1971. *Selected Writings,* Vol. II: *Word and Language*. The Hague and Paris: Mouton.

_____. 1971a. "The Kazan' School of Polish Linguistics and its Place in the International Development of Phonology", Jakobson 1971:394-428.

_____. 1971b. "Značenie Kruševskogo v razvitii nauki o jazyke", Jakobson 1971:429-50.

_____. 1971c. "The Phonemic and Grammatical Aspects of Language in their Interrelations", Jakobson 1971:103-14.

_____, and J. Lotz. 1949. "Notes on the French Phonemic Pattern". *Word* 5.151-58.

Jarceva, V. N., et al., eds. 1969. *Edinicy raznyx urovnej grammatičeskogo stroja jazyka i ix vzaimodejstvie*. Moscow.

Jones, D. 1957. *The History and Meaning of the Term "Phoneme"*. London.

Joos, M., ed. [4]1967, [1]1957. *Readings in Linguistics* I: *The Development of Descriptive Linguistics in America 1925-56*. Chicago: U. of Chicago Press.

Joshi, D. N. 1975. "Morphophonemic Alternations". *International Journal of Dravidian Linguistics* 4.278-82.

Karcevskij, S. 1931. "Sur la phonologie de la phrase". *TCLP* 4.188-227.

Kats, J. 1939. *Het phonologisch en morphonologisch System van het roermondsch Dialect*. Roermond, Maasiek: J. J. Romen & Zonen.

Kenstowicz, M. 1975. "Rule-Application in Pre-Generative American Phonology". *The Transformational-Generative Paradigm and Modern Linguistic Theory*, ed. by E. F. K. Koerner, 145-72. Amsterdam: John Benjamins.

Kiparsky, P. 1968a. "Linguistic Universals and Linguistic Change", *Universals in Linguistic Theory*, ed. by E. Bach and R. T. Harms, 170-202. New York: Holt, Rinhart and Winston.

_____. 1968b. "How Abstract is Phonology?" (mimeographed paper.) Indiana University Linguistics Club. (Repr. 1973 in *Three Dimensions of Linguistic Theory*, ed. by O. Fujimura. Tokyo: TEC Company.

Kisseberth, C. W. 1969. "On the Abstractness of Phonology: the Evidence from Yawelmani". *Papers in Linguistics* 1.248-82.

Kloster-Jensen, M. 1973. Review in English of Haslev 1972. *Norsk Tidsskrift for Sprogvidenskap* 27.165-69.

Koerner, E. F. K. 1972a. Review of Häusler 1968. *Linguistics* 77.63-76.

_____. 1972b. "Jan Baudouin de Courtenay: His Place in the History of Linguistic Science". *Canadian Slavonic Papers* 14.663-83.

_____. 1972c. "Hermann Paul and Synchronic Linguistics". *Lingua* 29. 274-307.

_____. 1973a. *Ferdinand de Saussure: Origin and Development of his Linguistic Theory in Western Studies of Language*. Braunschweig: Vieweg. (2nd printing, 1974.)

_____. 1973b. Review of Baudouin de Courtenay 1972. *Language Sciences* 27.45-49.

Kômarek, M. 1964. "Sur l'appréciation fonctionelle des alternances morphonologiques". *Travaux linguistiques de Prague* 1.145-61.

Kruszewski, M. 1880. "Lingvističeskie zametki". *RFV* 4.35-62.

_____. 1881a. *K voprosu o gune: Issledovanie v oblasti staroslavjanskogo vokalizma* (= *RFV* 5.1-109.)

_____. 1881b. *Über die Lautabwechslung*. Kazan: Universitätsbuchdruckerei.

_____. 1882. "Otvet g. Brückner'u". *RFV* 7.135-39.

_____. 1883. *Očerk nauki o jazyke*. Kazan.

_____. 1884-90. *Principien der Sprachentwicklung* (= *Techmers Internationale Zeitschrift für allgemeine Sprachwissenschaft* 1884.295-307; 1885.258-68; 1886.145-87; 1889-90.133-44, 339-60.) (Tr. of Kruszewski 1883.)

_____. 1967. *Wybór pism*, ed. and tr. by J. Kuryłowicz and K. Pomorska, with intro. by J. Kuryłowicz and R. Jakobson. Breslau, Warsaw, Cracow.

Kukenheim, L. 1951. *Contributions à l'histoire de la grammaire grecque, latine et hébraïque à l'époque de la renaissance*. Leiden.

Kuryłowicz, J. 1967. "Phonologie und Morphonologie", in Hamm 1967.

_____. 1968. "The Notion of Morpho(pho)neme", Lehmann and Malkiel 1968:65-81.

Langendoen, D. T. 1968. *The London School of Linguistics*. Cambridge, Mass.: MIT Press.

Lamb, S. M. 1964. "On Alternation, Transformation, Realization, and Stratification". *Georgetown University Monograph Series on Languages and Linguistics* 17.105-22.

_____. 1966a. *Outline of Stratificational Grammar*. Washington, D.C.: Georgetown U. P.

_____. 1966b. "Prolegomena to a Theory of Phonology". *Lg* 42.536-73.

Lehmann, W. P., and Y. Malkiel, eds. 1968. *Directions for Historical Linguistics: A Symposium*. Austin and London: U. of Texas Press.

Leont'ev, A. A. 1961. "I. A. Boduèn de Kurtenè i peterburgskaja škola russkoj lingvistiki". *VJ* No. 4.116-24.

_____. 1966. "Boduèn i francuzskaja lingvistika". *Izvestija AN SSSR, Serija literatury i jazyka* 25.331ff.

Leopold, W. F. 1948. "German ch". *Lg* 24.179-80. (Repr. in *RIL*, 215-16.)

Leskien, A. 1884. *Der Ablaut der Wurzelsilben im Litauischen* (= *Abhandlungen der philologisch-historischen Classe der Königl. Sächsischen Gesellschaft der Wissenschaften*, Vol. 9, No. 4.) Leipzig.

_____. ⁹1969. *Handbuch der altbulgarischen (altkirchenslavischen) Sprache*. Heidelberg.

Lightner, T. M. 1970. "On Swadesh and Voegelin's 'A Problem in Phonological Alternation'". *Papers in Linguistics* 3.201-20.

Lopatin, V. V., and I. S. Uluxanov. 1969. "K sootnošeniju edinic slovoobrazovanija i morfonologii", Jarceva 1969:119-32.

Lounsbury, F. G. 1953. "The Method of Descriptive Morphology", *Oneida Verb Morphology* (= *Yale University Publications in Anthropology*, 48.) (Repr. in *RIL*, 379-85.)

Lyons, J. 1962. "Phonemic and Nonphonemic Phonology: Some Typological Reflections". *IJAL* 28.127-34.

Makaev, E. A., and E. S. Kubrjakova. 1967. "O predmete i zadačax morfonologii i ee meste sredi drugix lingvističeskix disciplin", *Soviet Contributions to the Soviet-Čekoslovak Symposium 18-22 April 1967*, 3-34. Moscow.

_____. 1969. "O statuse morfonologii i edinicax ee opisanija", Jarceva 1969:87-119.

Malone, J. L. 1966. "Old Irish Morphophonemics and Ordered Process Rules". *Lingua* 16.238-54.

Marchand, J. W. 1956. "Internal Reconstruction of Phonemic Split". *Lg* 32.245-53.

Martin, S. E. 1952. *Morphophonemics of Standard Colloquial Japanese* (= *Language Dissertations*, 47.) Baltimore, Md.: Linguistic Society of America.

_____. 1954. *Korean Morphophonemics* (= *William Dwight Whitney Linguistic Series*, 12.) Baltimore, Md.: Linguistic Society of America.

Martinet, A. 1936. "Neutralisation et archiphonème". *TCLP* 6.46-57.

_____. 1949a. *Phonology as Functional Phonetics* (= *Publications of the Philological Society*, 15.) London: Oxford U. P.

_____. 1949b. "About Structural Sketches". *Word* 5.13-35.

_____. 1960. *Eléments de linguistique générale*. Paris: Armand Colin.

_____. 1965. "De la morphonologie". *La linguistique* 1.15-30.

Matthews, P. H. 1965a. "Some Concepts in Word and Paradigm Morphology". *Foundations of Language* 1.268-89.

_____. 1965b. "The Inflectional Component of a Word-and-Paradigm Grammar". *Journal of Linguistics* 1.139-71.

_____. 1972. *Inflectional Morphology*. Cambridge: Cambridge U. P.

_____. 1974. *Morphology: An Introduction to the Theory of Word Structure* (= *Cambridge Textbooks in Linguistics,* 1.) Cambridge: Cambridge U. P.

Mathesius, V. 1965. "Kuda my prišli v jazykoznanii", *Istorija jazykoznanija XIX. i XX. vekov v očerkax i izvlečenijax*, Vol. 2, ed. by V. A. Zvegincev, 141-46. Moscow.

McCawley, J. D. 1967. "Sapir's Phonologic Representation". *IJAL* 33.106-11.

McQuown, N. A. 1976. "American Indian Linguistics in New Spain", *American Indian Languages and American Linguistics,* ed. by W. L. Chafe, 105-27. Lisse: Peter de Ridder Press.

Meillet, A. 1903. *Introduction à l'étude comparative des langues indo-européennes*. Paris.

_____. 1906. *Les alternances vocaliques en vieux slave* (= *Mémoires de la société de linguistique de Paris* 14.193-209, 332-90.)

_____. 1930. Obituary of Baudouin de Courtenay. *Revue des études slaves* 10.174-75.

_____, and A. Vaillant. 1924. *Grammaire de la langue serbo-croate*. Paris.

_____, and H. de Willman-Grabowsky. 1921. *Grammaire de la langue polonaise*. Paris.

Misra, V. N. 1964. "The Structural Framework of Pāṇini's Linguistic Analysis of Sanskrit", *Proceedings of the 9th International Congress of Linguists,* ed. by H. G. Lunt, 743-47. The Hague: Mouton.

Misra, V. N. 1966. *The Descriptive Technique of Pāṇini: An Introduction.* The Hague: Mouton.

Neisser, F. 1935. *Die Reduplikation im Georgischen.* Dr. phil. diss., Universität Wien.

Newman, P. 1968. "The Reality of Morphophonemes". *Lg* 44.507-15.

Newman, S. 1944. *Yokuts Language of California* (= *Viking Fund Publications in Anthropology,* 2.) New York.

Nida, E. A. ¹1946, ²1949. *Morphology: The Descriptive Analysis of Words.* Ann Arbor: U. of Michigan Press.

_____. 1948. "The Identification of Morphemes". *Lg* 24.414-41.

Ó Cuív, B. 1965. "Linguistic Terminology in the Medieval Irish Bardic Tracts". *TPS* 141-64.

Olmstead, D. L. 1951. "The Morphophonemics of Russian Noun Inflection". *SIL* 9.1-6.

Palmer, F. R., ed. 1970. *Prosodic Analysis.* London: Oxford U. P.

Paul, H. ²1886. *Prinzipien der Sprachgeschichte.* Halle.

Pike, K. L. 1947a. "Grammatical Prerequisites to Phonemic Analysis". *Wo* 3.155-72.

_____. 1947b. *Phonemics: A Technique for Reducing Languages to Writing.* Ann Arbor: U. of Michigan Press.

_____. 1952. "More on Grammatical Prerequisites". *Word* 8.106-21.

_____. ²1967. *Language in Relation to a Unified Theory of the Structure of Human Behavior.* The Hague: Mouton.

Polivanov, E. D. 1968. *Stat'i po obščemu jazykoznaniju.* Moscow.

Postal, P. M. 1964. "Boas and the Development of Phonology: Comments Based on Iroquoian". *IJAL* 30.269-80.

_____. 1968. *Aspects of Phonological Theory.* New York: Harper and Row.

Radlov, V. V. 1882. "Die Lautalternation und ihre Bedeutung für die Sprachentwicklung, belegt durch Beispiele aus den Türksprachen", *Abhandlungen des 5. Internat. Orientalisten-Congresses gehalten zu Berlin in 1881,* 54-70.

Red'kin, V. A. 1969. "O zadačax izučenija morfonologičeskix edinic v ix svjazi s edinicami smežnyx urovnej", *Jarceva* 1969:132-43.

Reformatskij, A. A. 1955. "O sootnošenii fonetiki i grammatiki (morfologii)", *Voprosy grammatičeskogo stroja,* 92-112. Moscow.

Reuschel, W. 1959. *Al-Ḥalīl ibn Aḥmad, der Lehrer Sībawaihis, als Grammatiker* (= *Mitteilungen des Instituts für Orientforschung,* 49.) Berlin: Akademie-Verlag.

Roberts, T. H. 1970. "Morphophonemics in a Stratificational Grammar". *Working Papers in Linguistics* 2.93-134.

Robins, R. H. 1951. *Ancient and Medieval Grammatical Theory in Europe*. London: G. Bell & Sons.

_____. 1957a. "Dionysius Thrax and the Western Grammatical Tradition". *TPS* 67-106. (Repr. in Robins 1970.)

_____. 1957b. "Aspects of Prosodic Analysis". *Proceedings of the University of Durham Philosophical Society,* Vol. 1, Ser. B (Arts), No. 1, 1-11. (Repr. in Robins 1970 and Palmer 1970.)

_____. 1959. "In Defense of WP". *TPS* 116-44. (Repr. in Robins 1970.)

_____. 1967. *A Short History of Linguistics*. Bloomington and London: Indiana U. P.

_____. 1970. *Diversions of Bloomsbury*. Amsterdam and London: North-Holland Publishing Co.

Rompelman, T. A. 1952. *Lambert ten Kate als Germanist (= Mededelingen der Koninklijke Nederlandse Akademie van Wetenschapen, Afd. Letterkunde, Nieuwe Reeks,* Deel 15, No. 9.) Amsterdam.

Sapir, E. 1921. *Language: An Introduction to the Study of Speech*. New York: Harcourt, Brace, and World.

_____. 1922. *The Takelma Language of Southwestern Oregon,* in *Handbook of American Indian Languages*, Pt. 2, ed. by F. Boas (= Bureau of American Ethnology, *Bulletin* 40.)

_____. 1925. "Sound Patterns in Language". *Lg* 1.37-51. (Repr. in Sapir 1949:33-45 and *RIL*, 19-25.)

_____. 1930. *The Southern Paiute Language (= Proceedings of the American Academy of Arts and Sciences,* 65.)

_____. 1933. "The Psychological Reality of Phonemes" (Repr. in Sapir 1949:46-60.)

_____. 1938. "Glottalized Continuants in Navaho, Nootka, and Kwakiutl". *Lg* 14.248-74. (Repr. in Sapir 1949:225-50.)

_____. 1949. *Selected Writings of Edward Sapir in Language, Culture, and Personality*, ed. by D. G. Mandelbaum. Berkeley and Los Angeles: U. of California Press.

_____, and H. Hoijer. 1967. *The Phonology and Morphology of the Navaho Language (= University of California Publications in Linguistics*, 50.) Berkeley and Los Angeles: U. of California Press.

_____, and M. Swadesh. 1939. *Nootka Texts: Tales and Ethnological Narratives with Grammatical Notes and Lexical Materials*. Philadelphia: Linguistic Society of America.

Saussure, F. de. 1879 [1878]. *Mémoire sur le système primitif des voyelles dans les langues indo-européennes*. Leipzig: Teubner. (Repr. 1968, Hildesheim: Olms.)

Saussure, F. de. ⁵1960. *Cours de linguistique générale.* Paris: Payot.

Scaglione, A. D. 1970. *Ars Grammatica.* The Hague and Paris: Mouton.

Schane, S. A. 1966. "The Morphophonemics of the French Verb". *Lg* 42.746-58.

_____. 1971. "The Phoneme Revisited". *Lg* 47.503-21.

_____. 1973. *Generative Phonology.* Englewood Cliffs, N.J.: Prentice-Hall.

Schogt, H. G. 1966. "Baudouin de Courtenay and Phonological Analysis". *La linguistique* 2.15-29.

Sebeok, T. A. 1943. "Vowel Morphophonemics of Hungarian Suffixes". *SIL* 2. 47-50.

Semaan, K. I. 1968. *Linguistics in the Middle Ages: Phonetics Studies in Early Islam.* Leiden: Brill.

Šaumjan, S. K. 1967. "Phonology and Generative Grammar", Hamm 1967:215-16.

_____. 1971. *Principles of Structural Linguistics.* The Hague: Mouton. (Tr. of *Strukturnaja lingvistika*, Moscow, 1965.)

Ščerba, L. V. 1912. *Russkie glasnye v kačestvennom i količestvennom otno-šenii.* St. Petersburg. (Repr. in *Izbrannie raboty po jazykoznaniju i fonetike*, Leningrad, 1958.)

Shapiro, M. 1974. "Morphophonemics as Semiotic". *Acta Linguistica Hafnien-sia* 15.29-50.

Shefts, B. 1961. *Grammatical Method in Pāṇini: His Treatment of Sanskrit Present Stems* (= *American Oriental Series, Essay* 1.) New Haven: American Oriental Society.

Silverstein, M. 1971. "Whitney on Language", in *Whitney on Language,* ed. by M. Silverstein. Cambridge, Mass. and London: MIT Press.

Smith, H. L., Jr. 1967. "The Concept of the Morphophone". *Lg* 43.306-41.

Sommerfelt, A. 1960. "Dichotomy in the Morphophonemic Vowel Alternations of Old Norse". *Norsk Tidsskrift for Sprogvidenskap* 19.327-36.

Staal, J. F. 1963. Review of Shefts 1961. *Lg* 39.483-88.

_____. 1965. "Context Sensitive Rules in Pāṇini". *Foundations of Language* 1.63-72.

_____. 1970. Review of Cardona 1969. *Lg* 46.502-7.

_____, ed. 1972. *A Reader on the Sanskrit Grammarians.* Cambridge, Mass.: MIT Press.

Stankiewicz, E. 1963. "Unity and Variety in the Morphophonemic Pattern of the Slavic Declensions", *American Contributions to the Fifth International Congress of Slavicists*, 83-105. The Hague: Mouton.

Stankiewicz, E. 1964. "Trubetzkoy and Slavic Morphophonemics". *Wiener Slavistisches Jahrbuch* 11.79-90.

_____. 1966. "Slavic Morphophonemics in its Typological and Diachronic Aspects", *Current Trends in Linguistics*, Vol. 3: *Theoretical Foundations*, ed. by T. A. Sebeok, 495-520. The Hague: Mouton.

_____. 1967. "Opposition and Hierarchy in Morphophonemic Alternations", *To Honor Roman Jakobson*, 1895-1905. The Hague: Mouton.

_____. 1976. *Baudouin de Courtenay and the Foundations of Structural Linguistics*. Lisse: Peter de Ridder Press. (Repr. of intro. to Baudouin de Courtenay 1972.)

Stanley, R. 1969. Review of Sapir and Hoijer 1967. *Lg* 45.927-39.

Stepanov, Ju. S. 1966. *Osnovy jazykoznanija*. Moscow.

Swadesh, M. 1934. "The Phonemic Principle". *Lg* 10.117-29. (Repr. in *RIL*, 32-37.)

_____, and C. F. Voegelin. 1939. "A Problem in Phonological Alternation". *Lg* 15.1-10. (Repr. in *RIL*, 88-92.)

Thomsen, V. 1927. *Geschichte der Sprachwissenschaft bis zum Ausgang des 19. Jahrhunderts*. Halle /Saale: M. Niemeyer.

Trager, G. L. 1934. "The Phonemes of Russian". *Lg* 10.334-44.

_____. 1944. "The Verb Morphology of Spoken French". *Lg* 20.131-41.

_____. 1955. "French Morphology: Verb Inflection". *Lg* 31.511-29.

_____, and H. L. Smith, Jr. 1951. *Outline of English Structure* (= *SIL*, *Occasional Papers*, 3.) Norman, Okla.: Battenburg Press.

Tritton, D. S. 1973. *Arabic*. London.

Trnka, B. 1961. "O morfonologické analogii". *Časopis pro moderní filologii* 43.65-73.

_____. 1967. "The Phonemic Organization of Morphemes", *Phonetica Pragensia*, ed. by M. Romportl and V. Skalička, 91-93. Prague.

Trubetzkoy, N. S. 1929a. *Polabische Studien* (= *Sitzungsberichte der Akademie der Wissenschaften in Wien, Philosophisch-historische Klasse*, Band 211.) Wien.

_____. 1929b. "Sur la 'morphonologie'". *TCLP* 1.85-88.

_____. 1931. "Gedanken über Morphonologie". *TCLP* 4.160-63.

_____. 1934. *Das morphonologische System der russischen Sprache* (= *TCLP* 5:2.)

_____. 1939. *Grundzüge der Phonologie* (= *TCLP* 8.) (Repr. 1958, Göttingen: Vandenhoeck & Ruprecht.)

_____. 1954. *Altkirchenslavische Grammatik*. Graz, Wien, Köln: Hermann Böhlaus Nachf.

Trubetzkoy, N. S. 1975. *N. S. Trubetzkoy's Letters and Notes,* prepared for publication by R. Jakobson. The Hague and Paris: Mouton.

Ułaszyn, H. 1927. "Klika uwag terminologicznych". *Prace filologiczne* 12. 405-15.

_____. 1931. "Laut, Phonema, Morphonema". *TCLP* 4.53-61.

Vachek, J. 1961. "A propos de la terminologie linguistique et du système de concepts linguistiques de l'Ecole de Prague". *Philologica Pragensia* 4.65-78.

_____. 1966. *The Linguistic School of Prague.* Bloomington and London: Indiana U. P.

Van Ginneken, J. 1934. "De phonologie van het Algemeen Nederlandsch". *Onze Taaltuin* 2.321-40.

Van Wijk, N. 1934. "Morphonologie". *De Nieuwe Taalgids* 28.112-17.

_____. 1939. *Phonologie: Een Hoofdstuk uit de structurelle Taalweten-schap.* The Hague: Martinus Nijhoff.

Voegelin, C. F. 1935. *Tübatulabal Grammar* (= *University of California Publications in American Archaeology and Ethnology* 34.55-190.)

_____. 1947. "A Problem in Morpheme Alternants and their Distribution". *Lg* 23.245-54.

Weijnen, A. 1944. "Morphologisch gekennmerkte phonemen". *Tijdschrift vor Nederlandse Taal- en Letterkunde* 63.198-213.

Weinreich, U., W. Labov, and M. I. Herzog. 1968. "Empirical Foundations for a Theory of Language Change", Lehmann and Malkiel 1968:97-188.

Wells, R. S. 1949. "Automatic Alternation". *Lg* 25.99-116.

Whitney, W. D. 1867. *Language and the Study of Language.* New York.

_____. 1875. *The Life and Growth of Language.* New York.

_____. 1884. "The Study of Hindu Grammar and the Study of Sanskrit". *American Journal of Philology* 5.279-97. (Repr. in *Whitney on Language,* ed. by M. Silverstein. Cambridge, Mass. and London: MIT Press.)

_____. [2]1889. *Sanskrit Grammar.*Cambridge, Mass.: Harvard U. P.

Whorf, B. L. 1942. "Language, Mind, and Reality". (Repr. in *Language, Thought, & Reality,* by B. L. Whorf. Cambridge, Mass.: MIT Press, 1956.)

Winteler, J. 1876. *Die Kerenzer Mundart des Kantons Glarus in ihren Grund-zügen dargestellt.* Leipzig and Heidelberg.

Wolfart, H. C. 1967. "Notes on the Early History of American Indian Lin-guistics". *Folia Linguistica* 1.153-71.

Worth, D. S. 1970. "On the Morphophonemics of the Slavic Verb". *Slavia* 39.1-9.

152   REFERENCES

Zimmer, K. E. 1970. "The Morphophonemics of Saussure's *Cours de linguistique général*". *Foundations of Language* 6.423-26.

Zwirner, E., and K. Zwirner. [2]1966. *Grundfragen der Phonometrie*. Basel and New York: S. Karger.

INDEX OF NAMES

Printed in the United States
706700001B